Math Skills
Made Easy

by
MYRL SHIREMAN

COPYRIGHT © 1999 Mark Twain Media, Inc.

ISBN 1-58037-094-2

Printing No. CD-1322

Mark Twain Media, Inc., Publishers
Distributed by Carson-Dellosa Publishing Company, Inc.

Art by ©Corel Corporation

TABLE OF CONTENTS

Introduction 1

ASSESSMENT ACTIVITIES **2**
   Assessment for Place Value 3
   Assessment for Addition 6
   Assessment for Subtraction 8
   Assessment for Multiplication 10
   Assessment for Division 13
   Assessment for Fractions 15
   Assessment for Decimals 18

TEACHER-DIRECTED ACTIVITIES **19**
   Understanding Place Value 19
   Understanding Exponents in Base Ten and Base Five 21
   Understanding Addition 25
   Understanding Subtraction 27
   Understanding Multiplication 29
   Understanding Division 32
   Understanding Fractions 35
   Understanding Decimals 50

INDEPENDENT ACTIVITIES **53**
   Learning About Place Value 53
   Learning About Exponents 56
   Learning About Base Five and Base Ten 58
   Review Lessons 59
   Learning About Addition 61
   More Addition Practice 63
   Learning About Subtraction..64
   Learning About Multiplication 68
   Learning About Division 71
   Learning About Fractions 74
   Learning About Decimals 87

ANSWER KEY **89**

INTRODUCTION

Middle school teachers and parents find that there is a wide range of proficiency among students in the basic mathematical operations that are required for success in mathematics at higher levels. Place value, fractions, and decimals are areas where the range of skill levels may be extreme.

A large number of middle school students have not mastered the mathematical processes associated with place value, fractions, and decimals because they have not had ample opportunity for extended skills practice. Other students have been introduced to these mathematical operations at an age when they were unable to understand the abstract concepts that were being presented. There is another group of students who can perform the mechanical steps required to solve a problem in fractions and decimals but cannot tell if the answer obtained is a realistic possibility.

Assessment to determine a student's level of understanding and specific teacher instruction to ensure the required skill is understood, followed by ample skills practice, will significantly increase the proficiency of many students. Therefore, this book is written with a strong emphasis on an initial assessment step to determine the level of understanding possessed by each student. **Assessment Activities** are provided to help the teacher determine where instruction should begin. A second important step for many students is the **Teacher-Directed Activities**. These activities are developed for the teacher to use with students who need direct instruction and close teacher observation as the skill is learned before any independent activities are assigned. Once the teacher has determined that the student has a grasp of the skill being taught, **Independent Activities** may be assigned to ensure ample practice. In some cases the teacher may determine that the students have the necessary understanding to handle the Independent Activities without Teacher-Directed Activities. The students simply need more practice, and the Teacher-Directed Activities are unnecessary.

The assignments in the book are designed so that students with short attention spans and other learning difficulties do not find the assignments overwhelming.

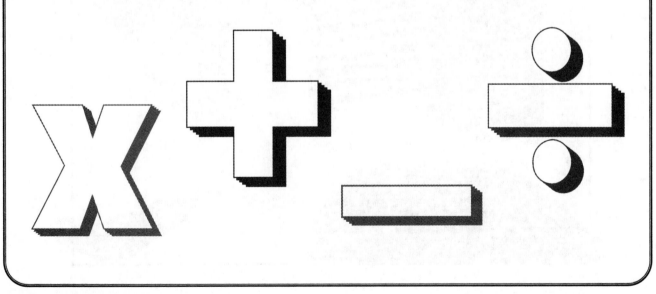

$125 + 300 = 425$ $750 - 400 = 350$ $5 \times (3 \times 7) = 3 \times (5 \times 7)$ $3/4 - 1/4 = 1/2$
$5 \times (3 \times 7) = 3 \times (5 \times 7)$ $3/4 - 1/4 = 1/2$ $125 + 300 = 425$ $750 - 400 = 350$

Assessment Activities

Before assigning activities in the book, it is important to determine the level of understanding possessed by each student. The following assessments are designed to be used to assess the student's mathematics skills and to determine where instruction should begin. Once the student level of understanding has been determined, it is advisable to teach the skills needed to complete the desired assignment in the Independent Activities Section. In administering the assessments, it is important to consider the attention span and any learning problems the students may possess. Administering the assessment in its entirety would be a questionable procedure for students who have experienced difficulty in learning mathematics. Each mathematics assessment may be used as a pretest and posttest item.

Name _____   Date _____

 Assessment for Place Value

Answer the following.

1. How many sticks in each bundle under the letter a?   _____
2. How many sticks in each bundle under the letter b?   _____
3. How many sticks in each bundle under the letter c?   _____
4. How many sticks in each bundle under the letter d?   _____
5. How many sticks in each bundle under the letter e?   _____

a. ||||||||| b. ||||||||| c. ||||||||| d. ||||||||| ||||||||| e. ||||||||| |||||||||

Answer the following problems.

6. 12 = _____ tens _____ ones   7. 18 = _____ tens _____ ones

8. 25 = _____ tens _____ ones   9, 84 = _____ tens _____ ones

10. 98 = _____ tens _____ ones

Rewrite each of the following as a number.

11. 10 + 3 = _____   12. 10 + 4 = _____   13. 70 + 3 = _____

14. 80 + 8 = _____   15. 90 + 9 = _____

Rewrite each of the following as a number.

16. 8 tens and 3 ones = _____   17. 6 tens and 6 ones = _____

18. 2 tens and 0 ones = _____   19. 8 tens and 0 ones = _____

20. 5 tens and 0 ones = _____   21. 7 tens and 1 one = _____

Rewrite each of the following as tens and ones.

22. 88 = _____ + _____   23. 36 = _____ + _____

24. 40 = _____ + _____   25. 97 = _____ + _____

Name _____   Date _____

Assessment for Place Value

Write the number for each statement.

26. twenty-three = _____ tens and _____ ones

27. forty-seven = _____ tens and _____ ones

28. seventy-eight = _____ tens and _____ ones

29. ninety = _____ tens and _____ ones

30. thirty = _____ tens and _____ ones

31. eighty-seven = _____ tens and _____ ones

Answer the following by writing the number of bundles of straws and individual straws needed to complete the blanks.

32. thirty-eight = _____ bundles of ten and _____ ones

33. sixty-three = _____ bundles of ten and _____ ones

34. ninety-six = _____ bundles of five and _____ ones

35. seventy = _____ bundles of ten and _____ ones

Answer the following.

36. Write the number that has 5 tens and 6 ones. _____

37. The number 74 has _____ tens and _____ ones.

38. Which of the following is the same as the number 39? Circle it.
    a. 30 + 7   b. 60 + 3   c. 30 + 8   d. 30 + 9   e. 80 + 7

39. Each of the numbers below has a circled numeral. Write the word for that number on the blank below each.
    a. ⑦6   b. ③5   c. 8⑧   d. ①9   e. ⑤4
    _____   _____   _____   _____   _____

40. In the blank write how many times greater the circled number is than the uncircled number.

    a. ③3 _____ times greater   b. ⑤5 _____ times greater

    c. ⑦7 _____ times greater   d. ⑧8 _____ times greater

    e. ⑨9 _____ times greater

Name _____ Date _____

Assessment for Place Value

41. Rewrite each of the following numbers in expanded form.

    a. 52 _____ + _____   b. 92 _____ + _____

    c. 87 _____ + _____   d. 99 _____ + _____

    e. 12 _____ + _____

42. Rewrite each of the following as a number without exponents.

    a. 3^2 = _____   b. 8^2 = _____   c. 5^3 = _____

    d. 2^5 = _____   e. 5^5 = _____

43. Rewrite each of the following as a number with an exponent.

    a. 4 = _____   b. 9 = _____   c. 64 = _____

    d. 16 = _____   e. 27 = _____   f. 216 = _____

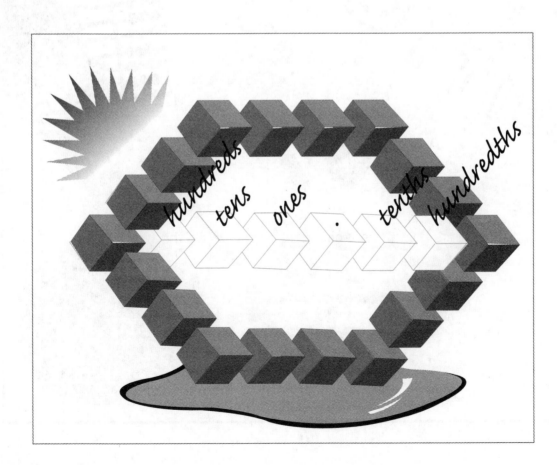

$$125 + 300 = 425 \quad 750 - 400 = 350 \quad 5 \times (3 \times 7) = 3 \times (5 \times 7) \quad 3/4 - 1/4 = 1/2$$
$$5 \times (3 \times 7) = 3 \times (5 \times 7) \quad 3/4 - 1/4 = 1/2 \quad 125 + 300 = 425 \quad 750 - 400 = 350$$

Assessment for Addition

Administer the following assessment to determine each student's mastery of the skills needed in addition at the middle school level. Many middle school students experience problems in addition because they have not mastered the addition facts, place value, and regrouping. The following problems will help determine the level of mastery attained by each student. Note the problems require students to apply addition facts and regroup from ones to tens, tens to hundreds, and hundreds to thousands.

Name _____ Date _____

Assessment for Addition Activities

Complete the following addition problems.

1. 9	2. 8	3. 7	4. 5	5. 6
+ 2	+ 9	+ 6	+ 6	+ 8

6. 5 + 3 = _____   7. 6 + 8 + 9 = _____

8. 7 + 8 + 4 = _____   9. 19 + 6 + 7 + 4 = _____

10. 78	11. 47	12. 78	13. 90	14. 87
+ 4	+ 43	+ 7	+ 57	+ 94

15. 41 + 62 + 83 + 52 = _____   16. 41 + 62 + 83 + 56 = _____

17. 238	18. 145	19. 345	20. 567	21. 467	22. 891	23. 234
+ 311	+ 534	+ 337	+ 338	+ 50	+ 239	+ 678

24. 546 + 278 + 789 = _____

125 + 300 = 4   750 - 400 = 350   5 x (3 x 7) = 3 x (5 x 7)   3/4 - 1/4 = 1/2
5 x (3 x 7) = 3 x (5 x 7)   125 + 300 = 425   750 - 400 = 350

Assessment for Subtraction

Administer the following assessment to determine each student's mastery of the skills needed in subtraction at the middle school level. Many middle school students experience problems in subtraction because they have not mastered the subtraction facts, place value, and regrouping. The following problems will help determine the level of mastery attained by each student. Note the problems require students to apply subtraction facts and regroup from tens to ones, hundreds to tens, and thousands to hundreds. It is important that students learn to check answers.

Name _____   Date _____

Assessment for Subtraction Activities

Complete the following subtraction problems.

1. 9
   - 2

2. 18
   - 9

3. 7
   - 6

4. 9 - 3 = _____

5. 29 - 8 = _____

6. 45 - 4 = _____

7. 21 - 11 = _____

8. 56 - 32 = _____

9. 35
   - 4

10. 56
    - 43

11. 78
    - 17

12. 57
    - 47

13. 94
    - 78

14. 38
    - 29

15. 56
    - 37

16. 87
    - 78

17. 234
    - 125

18. 568
    - 476

19. 4479
    - 2569

20. 5231
    - 4342

21. 67 - 58 = _____

22. 43 - 34 = _____

23. 456 - 267 = _____

24. 687 - 598 = _____

25. 5623 - 4734 = _____

125 + 300 = ~~ 25~~   750 - 400 = 350   5 x (3 x 7) = 3 x (5 x 7)   3/4 - 1/4 = 1/2
5 x (3 x 7) = 3 x ~~(5 x 7)~~   ~~3/4 - 1/4 = 1/2~~   ~~125 + 300 = 425~~   750 - 400 = 350

Assessment for Multiplication

First present the assessment with a one-minute time limit for each set of facts. Then present it as an untimed assessment. Compare the results for accuracy. Students who complete the basic facts assessment in one minute without errors have mastered the basic facts. Students who do not complete the multiplication assessment in the one-minute time limit but are accurate on the ones completed need more rote practice on the basic facts. These students can benefit from multiplication activities while practicing quick recall of the facts. Those who make errors on the work completed have a limited understanding of basic facts. Teaching of the basic facts must be the main thrust of instruction. It is not necessary to assess all students on each set. For example, it saves time to administer the 7's, 9's and 10's. Administer the total sets to those students who do not do well on the 7's, 9's and 10's.

Name _____ Date _____

 Assessment for Multiplication Part I

1. 2 x 1 = _____	37. 5 x 1 = _____	73. 8 x 1 = _____	109. 11 x 1 = ____
2. 2 x 2 = _____	38. 5 x 2 = _____	74. 8 x 2 = _____	110. 11 x 2 = ____
3. 2 x 3 = _____	39. 5 x 3 = _____	75. 8 x 3 = _____	111. 11 x 3 = ____
4. 2 x 4 = _____	40. 5 x 4 = _____	76. 8 x 4 = _____	112. 11 x 4 = ____
5. 2 x 5 = _____	41. 5 x 5 = _____	77. 8 x 5 = _____	113. 11 x 5 = ____
6. 2 x 6 = _____	42. 5 x 6 = _____	78. 8 x 6 = _____	114. 11 x 6 = ____
7. 2 x 7 = _____	43. 5 x 7 = _____	79. 8 x 7 = _____	115. 11 x 7 = ____
8. 2 x 8 = _____	44. 5 x 8 = _____	80. 8 x 8 = _____	116. 11 x 8 = ____
9. 2 x 9 = _____	45. 5 x 9 = _____	81. 8 x 9 = _____	117. 11 x 9 = ____
10. 2 x 10 = ____	46. 5 x 10 = ____	82. 8 x 10 = ____	118. 11 x 10 = ____
11. 2 x 11 = ____	47. 5 x 11 = ____	83. 8 x 11 = ____	119. 11 x 11 = ____
12. 2 x 12 = ____	48. 5 x 12 = ____	84. 8 x 12 = ____	120. 11 x 12 = ____

13. 3 x 1 = _____	49. 6 x 1 = _____	85. 9 x 1 = _____
14. 3 x 2 = _____	50. 6 x 2 = _____	86. 9 x 2 = _____
15. 3 x 3 = _____	51. 6 x 3 = _____	87. 9 x 3 = _____
16. 3 x 4 = _____	52. 6 x 4 = _____	88. 9 x 4 = _____
17. 3 x 5 = _____	53. 6 x 5 = _____	89. 9 x 5 = _____
18. 3 x 6 = _____	54. 6 x 6 = _____	90. 9 x 6 = _____
19. 3 x 7 = _____	55. 6 x 7 = _____	91. 9 x 7 = _____
20. 3 x 8 = _____	56. 6 x 8 = _____	92. 9 x 8 = _____
21. 3 x 9 = _____	57. 6 x 9 = _____	93. 9 x 9 = _____
22. 3 x 10 = ____	58. 6 x 10 = ____	94. 9 x 10 = ____
23. 3 x 11 = ____	59. 6 x 11 = ____	95. 9 x 11 = ____
24. 3 x 12 = ____	60. 6 x 12 = ____	96. 9 x 12 = ____

25. 4 x 1 = _____	61. 7 x 1 = _____	97. 10 x 1 = ____
26. 4 x 2 = _____	62. 7 x 2 = _____	98. 10 x 2 = ____
27. 4 x 3 = _____	63. 7 x 3 = _____	99. 10 x 3 = ____
28. 4 x 4 = _____	64. 7 x 4 = _____	100. 10 x 4 = ____
29. 4 x 5 = _____	65. 7 x 5 = _____	101. 10 x 5 = ____
30. 4 x 6 = _____	66. 7 x 6 = _____	102. 10 x 6 = ____
31. 4 x 7 = _____	67. 7 x 7 = _____	103. 10 x 7 = ____
32. 4 x 8 = _____	68. 7 x 8 = _____	104. 10 x 8 = ____
33. 4 x 9 = _____	69. 7 x 9 = _____	105. 10 x 9 = ____
34. 4 x 10 = ____	70. 7 x 10 = ____	106. 10 x 10 = ____
35. 4 x 11 = ____	71. 7 x 11 = ____	107. 10 x 11 = ____
36. 4 x 12 = ____	72. 7 x 12 = ____	108. 10 x 12 = ____

Name _____ Date _____

 Assessment for Multiplication Part II

1. 7	2. 8	3. 10	4. 14	5. 30	6. 51	7. 93	8. 63
x 4	x 9	x 6	x 2	x 9	x 8	x 2	x 3

 Assessment for Multiplication Part III

1.   8 x (3 x 5) = 8 x _____ = _____

2.   (4 x 3) x 2 = _____ x 2 = _____

3.   10 x (8 x 1) = 10 x _____ = _____

4.   (9 x 6) x 5 = _____ x _____ = _____

5.   10 x (3 x 9) = _____ x _____ = _____

6.   35 x (10 x 2) = _____ x _____ = _____

7.   (80 x 7) x 4 = _____ x _____ = _____

8.   (5 x 6) x (2 x 5) = _____ x _____ = _____

9.   (24 x 2) x (5 x 4) = _____ x _____ = _____

 Assessment for Multiplication Part IV

1.   5 x 28 = 5 (20 + 8) = 5 x 20 + 5 x 8 = _____ + _____ = _____

2.   6 x 35 = 6 (_____ + _____) = 6 x _____ + 6 x _____ = _____ + _____ = _____

3.   8 x 89 = _____ (_____ + _____) = 8 x _____ + 8 x _____ = _____ + _____ = _____

4.   7 x 340 = _____ (_____ + _____) = 7 x _____ + 7 x _____ = _____ + _____ = _____

5.   4 x 548 = _____ (_____ + _____ + _____) = 4 x _____ + 4 x _____ + 4 x _____ =

     _____ + _____ + _____ = _____

Assessment for Multiplication Part V

1. 14	2. 34	3. 56	4. 66	5. 234	6. 732	7. 789	8. 2345
x 5	x 8	x 15	x 64	x 63	x 40	x 301	x 435

12

Name _____   Date _____

125 + 300 = 4~~   750 - 400 = 350   5 x (3 x 7) = 3 x (5 x 7)   3/4 - 1/4 = 1/2
5 x (3 x 7) = 3 x (5 x ~   ~~ ~~   125 ~~ 425   750 - 400 = 350

Assessment for Division

 Assessment for Division Part I

1. $2\overline{)10}$ 2. $5\overline{)10}$ 3. $6\overline{)18}$ 4. $9\overline{)36}$

5. $6\overline{)12}$ 6. $5\overline{)75}$ 7. $4\overline{)36}$ 8. $3\overline{)72}$

9. $6 \div 2 =$ _____   10. $24 \div 3 =$ _____   11. $42 \div 7 =$ _____   12. $88 \div 8 =$ _____

13. $144 \div 6 =$ _____   14. $24 \div 8 =$ _____   15. $49 \div 7 =$ _____   16. $120 \div 3 =$ _____

17. $5\overline{)155}$ 18. $4\overline{)176}$ 19. $3\overline{)777}$ 20. $7\overline{)329}$

21. $5\overline{)105}$ 22. $6\overline{)630}$ 23. $3\overline{)330}$ 24. $7\overline{)490}$

Name _____ Date _____

Assessment for Division Part II

1. $65\overline{)390}$ 2. $38\overline{)266}$ 3. $23\overline{)506}$ 4. $15\overline{)405}$

5. $14\overline{)308}$ 6. $14\overline{)560}$ 7. $15\overline{)315}$ 8. $17\overline{)663}$

9. $34\overline{)782}$ 10. $16\overline{)400}$ 11. $27\overline{)216}$ 12. $31\overline{)124}$

13. $36\overline{)828}$ 14. $18\overline{)792}$ 15. $15\overline{)750}$ 16. $20\overline{)980}$

17. $600\overline{)900}$ 18. $119\overline{)476}$ 19. $120\overline{)880}$ 20. $141\overline{)999}$

21. $314\overline{)7222}$ 22. $236\overline{)2832}$ 23. $457\overline{)1265}$ 24. $132\overline{)4625}$

Name _____ Date _____

125 + 300 = 4~~ ~~ 750 - 400 = 350   5 x (3 x 7) = 3 x (5 x 7)   3/4 - 1/4 = 1/2
5 x (3 x 7) = 3 x (5 x ~~ ~~   ~~ ~~   ~~ ~~ = ~~ ~~   125 + ~~ ~~ = ~~ ~~ 5   750 - 400 = 350

Assessment for Fractions

1. What fractional part of the circle is shaded?

$\frac{1}{2}$ $\frac{1}{3}$ $\frac{2}{3}$ $\frac{3}{4}$

2. What fractional part of the circle is shaded?

$\frac{1}{2}$ $\frac{1}{3}$ $\frac{2}{3}$ $\frac{3}{4}$

3. What fractional part of the circle is shaded?

$\frac{1}{2}$ $\frac{1}{3}$ $\frac{2}{3}$ $\frac{3}{4}$

4. What fractional part of the circle is shaded?

$\frac{3}{5}$ $\frac{5}{8}$ $\frac{1}{2}$ $\frac{2}{3}$

5. What fractional part of the circle is shaded?

$\frac{3}{5}$ $\frac{5}{8}$ $\frac{1}{2}$ $\frac{2}{3}$

6. Divide the following diagram into halves.

7. Divide the following into thirds.

8. Divide the following into fourths.

9. Divide the following into sixths.

10. On the blanks below arrange the following fractions from largest to smallest.

$\frac{1}{8}$ $\frac{1}{2}$ $\frac{1}{3}$ $\frac{1}{4}$ $\frac{1}{6}$ $\frac{1}{16}$

____   ____   ____   ____   ____   ____

11. Circle the numerator for each of the following fractions.

$\frac{1}{8}$ $\frac{1}{2}$ $\frac{1}{3}$ $\frac{1}{4}$ $\frac{1}{6}$ $\frac{9}{16}$

Name _____   Date _____

$125 + 300 = 4$ $750 - 400 = 350$ $5 \times (3 \times 7) = 3 \times (5 \times 7)$ $3/4 - 1/4 = 1/2$
$5 \times (3 \times 7) = 3 \times (5 \times 7)$ Assessment for Fractions $125 + 300 = 425$ $750 - 400 = 350$

12. Circle the denominator for each of the following fractions.

$\frac{1}{8}$ $\frac{1}{2}$ $\frac{1}{3}$ $\frac{1}{4}$ $\frac{1}{6}$ $\frac{9}{16}$ $\frac{2}{4}$ $\frac{3}{16}$ $\frac{4}{8}$ $\frac{8}{16}$

13. Circle the fractions below that equal one-half ($\frac{1}{2}$).

$\frac{2}{4}$ $\frac{3}{16}$ $\frac{4}{8}$ $\frac{8}{16}$

14. Circle below the fractions that equal one-fourth ($\frac{1}{4}$).

$\frac{12}{16}$ $\frac{24}{32}$ $\frac{3}{8}$ $\frac{1}{8}$ $\frac{3}{4}$

15. Circle the fractions that equal six-eighths ($\frac{6}{8}$).

$\frac{12}{16}$ $\frac{24}{32}$ $\frac{3}{8}$ $\frac{1}{8}$ $\frac{3}{4}$

16. Circle the fractions that equal one-sixteenth ($\frac{1}{16}$).

$\frac{12}{16}$ $\frac{24}{32}$ $\frac{3}{8}$ $\frac{1}{8}$ $\frac{12}{48}$

Circle the simplified fractions for each improper fraction.

17. $\frac{2}{4} =$ a. $\frac{1}{2}$ b. $\frac{3}{4}$ c. $\frac{1}{3}$ d. $\frac{5}{8}$

18. $\frac{4}{10} =$ a. $\frac{1}{2}$ b. $\frac{2}{5}$ c. $\frac{5}{6}$ d. $\frac{3}{8}$

19. $\frac{6}{8} =$ a. $\frac{2}{5}$ b. $\frac{1}{2}$ c. $\frac{3}{4}$ d. $\frac{7}{8}$

20. $\frac{4}{16} =$ a. $\frac{3}{4}$ b. $\frac{1}{5}$ c. $\frac{1}{8}$ d. $\frac{1}{4}$

21. Add the following fractions.

a. $\frac{3}{4}$ b. $\frac{5}{8}$ c. $\frac{5}{16}$ d. $\frac{1}{2}$ e. $\frac{3}{8}$
   $+\frac{1}{4}$ $+\frac{2}{8}$ $+\frac{4}{16}$ $+\frac{1}{3}$ $+\frac{2}{4}$

22. Subtract the following fractions.

a. $\frac{3}{8}$ b. $\frac{5}{6}$ c. $\frac{9}{16}$ d. $\frac{1}{2}$ e. $\frac{5}{8}$
   $-\frac{2}{8}$ $-\frac{3}{6}$ $-\frac{6}{16}$ $-\frac{1}{3}$ $-\frac{3}{16}$

Name _____   Date _____

Assessment for Fractions

23. Multiply the following fractions.

   a. $\frac{1}{3} \times \frac{2}{3} =$ b. $\frac{3}{8} \times \frac{1}{2} =$ c. $\frac{3}{5} \times \frac{2}{3} =$

24. Divide the following fractions.

   a. $\frac{1}{3} \div \frac{2}{3} =$ b. $\frac{3}{8} \div \frac{1}{2} =$ c. $\frac{3}{5} \div \frac{2}{3} =$

25. Circle the improper fractions in the group below.

   $\frac{7}{6}$ $\frac{3}{7}$ $\frac{3}{2}$ $\frac{9}{8}$ $\frac{3}{4}$ $\frac{5}{4}$ $\frac{1}{2}$ $\frac{6}{7}$ $\frac{8}{10}$ $\frac{4}{3}$

26. Circle the mixed numbers in the following groups.

   a. $1\frac{7}{8}$ $\frac{7}{6}$ $3\frac{1}{2}$ $\frac{3}{2}$ $2\frac{2}{3}$ $\frac{3}{4}$

   b. $\frac{5}{4}$ $\frac{1}{2}$ $5\frac{3}{4}$ $\frac{8}{10}$ $\frac{4}{3}$ $3\frac{2}{5}$

27. Change the following mixed numbers into improper fractions.

   a. $1\frac{2}{3}$ b. $3\frac{1}{2}$ c. $2\frac{3}{4}$

28. Change the following improper fractions to mixed numbers.

   a. $\frac{7}{6}$ _____   b. $\frac{9}{5}$ _____   c. $\frac{16}{9}$ _____

29. Add the following improper fractions. Simplify the answers.

   a. $\frac{4}{3}$
      $+\frac{5}{3}$

   b. $\frac{3}{2}$
      $+\frac{4}{2}$

   c. $\frac{7}{6}$
      $+\frac{1}{6}$

30. Subtract the following improper fractions. Simplify the answers.

   a. $\frac{5}{3}$
      $-\frac{4}{3}$

   b. $\frac{8}{5}$
      $-\frac{6}{5}$

   c. $\frac{9}{6}$
      $-\frac{3}{2}$

31. Multiply the following improper fractions. Simplify the answers.

   a. $\frac{3}{2} \times \frac{5}{2} =$ b. $\frac{5}{3} \times \frac{2}{3} =$ c. $\frac{5}{3} \times \frac{3}{2} =$

Name _____   Date _____

125 + 300 = 42~~~~~ 750 - 400 = 350   5 x (3 x 7) = 3 x (5 x 7)   3/4 - 1/4 = 1/2
5 x (3 x 7) = 3 x (5 x 7)   ~~~~~ Assessment for Decimals ~~~~ 5   750 - 400 = 350

Write the decimal for each statement.

1. Three tenths _____   4. Five thousandths _____

2. Five hundredths _____   5. one hundred sixty-five thousandths _____

3. Thirty-five hundredths _____

Place the decimal point properly in the following numbers

6. Six-tenths   0 6   9. Two and forty-five hundredths   0 2 4 5

7. Five hundredths   0 0 5   10. Three thousandths   0 0 0 3

8. One and five tenths   0 1 5   11. One hundred twenty-six thousandths   0 1 2 6

Circle the decimal that equals the fraction

12. $\frac{1}{2}$ =   0.50   0.6   1.4

13. $\frac{3}{4}$ =   0.8   0.75   4.6

14. $\frac{2}{5}$ =   0.4   0.56   2.34

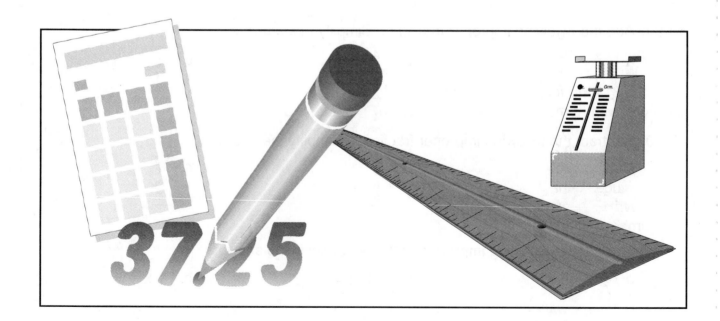

125 + 300 = 4~~2 5~~   750 - 400 = 350   5 x (3 x 7) = 3 x (5 x 7)   3/4 - 1/4 = 1/2
5 x (3 x 7) = 3 x (~~5 x 7~~) ~~1/4~~   ~~1/4 = 1/2~~   ~~125 + 300 = 425~~   750 - 400 = 350

Teacher-Directed Activities

To the teacher: Middle school students experience difficulty in mathematics if they do not understand place value. In middle school many students will have a firm grasp of place value. For these students, some of the suggested teaching exercises below are unnecessary. However, a large number of middle school students do not understand place value and, as a result, experience difficulty in mathematics. It is important to determine the level of understanding the student has and make sure that any misunderstandings are corrected.

Understanding Place Value

The following exercises are designed to use with students prior to assigning independent work. In determining which exercises to use, the teacher will have to determine the level of understanding of the student. The assessments found in the book may be used to determine the student's level of understanding.

Write numbers like the following on the board or overhead. Any two-digit numbers are acceptable for the exercise. 25   39   46   52   67   78   83   91

1. When you point to a number, have the students tell you the number name.

2. See if students can identify the number name when using the following type of statements. "Name the number that has three tens and nine ones."

More About Place Value

If students can complete the requirements for the exercises above, continue with the following. Write a number like 38 on the board. Have students tell the number of tens and ones. Then have the students tell what number the 3 stands for.

Write 30. How many tens in 30? So the 3 in 38 really means the number 30? What does the 8 stand for? So 38 means 3 tens or 30 and 8 ones. So 30 (3 tens) + 8 (ones) is 38. Continue with numbers like 25, 39, 46, 52, 67, 78, 83, and 91.

Write 25 on the board. Have the students tell you the number of tens in 25. Write the number 20 in the form 25 = 20 + _____. Then ask the students to tell how many ones in the number 25. Write the number 5 in the form 25 = 20 + 5. Write the words "expanded notation" on the board. Tell the students that 25 written in expanded notation is 20 + 5.

Write the numbers 25   39   46   52   67   78   83   91 on the board or overhead. Write the numbers in expanded notation without teacher direction.

Checking Understanding of Place Value

This exercise is designed so the teacher can double check students' understanding before independent work.

Let's change the 3 in 38 to 4. What number do we have? How many tens? How many ones? So the 4 in 48 really means the number _____? What does the 8 stand for? So 48 means _____ tens and _____ ones. So what number can I write on the board that the numeral 4 stands for? Write 40 + _____ on the board. How many ones go in the blank? Write 40 + 8 = 48. Have students verbalize 4 tens equals 40 plus 8 ones equals 48. Continue with numbers like 25, 39, 46, 52, 67, 78, 83, and 91.

Understanding Place Value for Numbers Greater than 99

Review place value for numbers like 36, 78, and 94. Use questions that touch on the understandings developed in the previous exercises.

Write numbers like the following on the board or overhead. Any three-digit numbers are acceptable for the exercise. 131 267 345 569 684 721 822 989

1. Point to a number and have the students tell you the number name.

2. See if students can identify the number name when using the following type of statements. "Name the number that has three hundreds, four tens, and five ones." If students demonstrate an understanding, move on to the following exercises.

Write a number like 581 on the board. Have students tell the number of hundreds, tens, and ones. Then have the students tell what number the 5 stands for, the number 8, and the number 1.

Write 500 on the overhead or board. How many hundreds in this number? tens? So the 5 in 500 really stands for the number (500 or 5 hundreds)? What does the 8 stand for? So the 8 really is the number? (80) So 581 means 5 hundreds or 500 and 8 tens or 80, and 1 one. So (5 hundreds or 50 tens) + 8 (tens or 80) + 1 (one) = 581

Continue with numbers like 251, 296, 468, 520, 679, 786, 835, and 910. Make certain students understand how to identify the place value of each number. This is the time when the teacher determines if the students are ready for the independent activities.

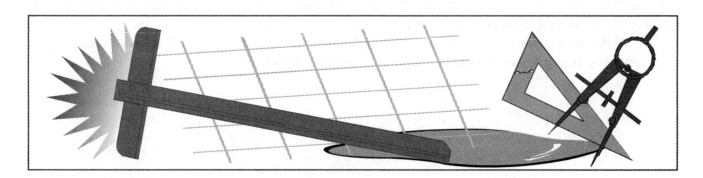

125 + 300 = 425   750 - 400 = 350   5 x (3 x 7) = 3 x (5 x 7)   3/4 - 1/4 = 1/2
5 x (3 x 7) = 3 x (5 x 7)   3/4 - 1/4 = 1/2   125 + 300 = 425   750 - 400 = 350
Teacher-Directed Activities

Understanding Exponents in Base Ten

Write the number 4 on the board or overhead. Ask the students what two numbers must be multiplied to get the number 4. Write _____ x _____ = 4 on the board and have students tell what two numbers should go on the blanks. After students have suggested 2 as the number, write the number 2 on the blanks. Tell the students they will learn a new way to write 2 x 2 = 4. Write $2^2 = 4$ on the board or overhead. Tell the students that 2^2 is read as "two to the second power." The large 2 is called the **base number**. The small 2 is called an **exponent**. The exponent tells how many times the base number is to be multiplied.

Write 3^2 on the board or overhead. Ask the students which is the base number and which is the exponent. Have the students tell you what the exponent tells you to do. Then write 3 x 3 = 9. Indicate that 3^2 is "three to the second power or 3 squared," which is 9.

Continue the above lesson with the numbers 9, 16, 27, 32, 64, and 125. Each time, have the students name the base number and exponent number. Have the students tell you what the exponent tells them to do. Show them that numbers like 16 might be written 4^2 or 2^4. Have the students verbalize what the exponents indicate should be performed. Have the students write out 4 x 4 = 16 and 2 x 2 x 2 x 2 = 16.

Students need experience with the numbers 10^0 10^1 10^2 10^3. Students must understand that, except for zero, any number raised to the **zero** power equals 1. A number raised to the first power is that number ($10^1 = 10$). A number raised to the second power is the number multiplied by itself. A number raised to the third power is the number multiplied three times, and so on.

Go over the following until students understand how the exponents affect the base numbers. $10^0 = 1$, $10^1 = 10$, $10^2 = 10 \times 10 = 100$, $10^3 = 10 \times 10 \times 10 = 1000$. Then have students solve 10^4 and 10^5 under teacher direction.

Have students solve 2^0, 2^1, 2^2, 2^3, and 2^4 with teacher supervision to double check understanding.

Understanding Exponents in Base Five and Base Ten

Many students can develop a better understanding of place value by exploring another number system. Before doing that, it is important to review Base Ten. Make certain the students review how place value works. An overhead projector can be very effective when presenting the diagram with straws. On a transparency sheet draw a full-page copy of Diagram I and II below.

Use 10 individual straws, 10 bundles of 10 straws, and one bundle of 100 straws to present the concept in a concrete manner. Indicate that you have one of something. Each time you place a numeral on Diagram I, place the required number of straws on Diagram II. Ask the students where the 1 should be placed in a Base Ten system. Continue with 2, 3, 4, 5, 6, 7, 8, and 9. Then present the number 10. Each time, write the numeral on Diagram I and place the same number of straws on Diagram II. Make sure students see the relationship. Then, when the number is 10, replace the 10 ones with a bundle of 10 straws and place the bundle under the tens column. Write the number 10 on Diagram I with 1, in the tens column and 0 in the ones column). Indicate that one bundle of 10 straws is the same as 10 ones. Continue with the numerals 1, 2, 3, 4, 5, 6, 7, 8, and 9 in the ones column in Diagram I and straws on Diagram II and have students tell what the number is and how many tens and ones the number represents. When 10 individual straws are in the ones column, the students should see that the 10 are again traded for another bundle of 10 straws that are in the tens column. Write the number 20 in Diagram I. Discuss with the students the importance of the zero in the ones column. The zero indicates no straws are in the ones column. Discuss zero as a place holder. If students are experiencing difficulty, continue with the straws in Diagram II and the corresponding numerals in Diagram I.

Many times students will understand the Base Ten concept following the above teaching procedure using straws. If so, discontinue using the straws and Diagram II and continue using Diagram I. Continue with 21, 22, 23, 24, 25, 26, 27, 28, and 29. Now ask the students what will happen when the number is 30. If students can tell you the 10 ones should be recorded as another 10 in the tens column, continue as follows.

What happens when there is a 9 in the tens column and 10 more ones are added? Students should see that 10 tens is 100. A bundle of 100 straws is placed on Diagram II, and the numeral 1 is placed in the hundreds column of Diagram I. Zeros should be placed in the tens and ones columns.

Diagram I

Thousands	Hundreds	Tens	Ones

Diagram II

Thousands	Hundreds	Tens	Ones

Place the number 899 on Diagram I with the numeral 8 under the hundreds and 9s in the tens and ones columns. Now indicate that one more is added to the ones column. Do students understand **why** the tens column and ones column become zero and the hundreds column becomes 9?

As a final review, write the number 299 on the overhead. Ask the students to tell you how many ones, tens, and hundreds are in the number. Then add one more and see if students can write the new number. Ask them what each numeral means in the new number. Remind them of the importance of zero in the Base Ten system.

Write the following on the overhead or board. Have students tell you what number each base and exponent represents. Write the number on the blank below each base and exponent. Then have the students tell you how many times greater the tens is than the ones, the hundreds is than the tens, and the thousands is than the hundreds. Write the answer on the second blank so students can see the answer.

	Thousands	Hundreds	Tens	Ones
	10^3	10^2	10^1	10^0
Number:	_____	_____	_____	_____
Times greater:	_____	_____	_____	

For the next exercise, Base Five is chosen. Another base could have been chosen, but Base Five is very adequate to solidify the concept of place value in the minds of the students. An understanding of Base Five indicates a grasp of the place value concept.

Write the numerals 4, 3, 2, 1, and 0 on the board or overhead. Tell the students you are going to introduce a new number system. In this new system the only numerals used are those on the overhead. Tell the students the numbers written for this system will be written with a subscript. The subscript will be the numeral 5. The number 10_5 is read as "one zero Base Five." Have the students read the following Base Five numbers.

10_5: one-zero, Base Five (stress the number is not ten)
11_5: one-one, Base Five (stress the number is not eleven)
12_5: one-two, Base Five (stress the number is not twelve)
Make sure students know that the subscript 5 will indicate **Base Five**.

On a transparency sheet draw a full-page copy of Diagram I and II on the next page

Use five individual straws, five bundles of five straws, and one bundle of 125 straws to present the concept in a concrete manner. Begin to place the straws in the ones column one at a time while commenting "one, two, three, four." Each time you place a numeral on Diagram I, place the required number of straws on Diagram II. Ask the students where the ones should be placed in a Base Five system. Then present the number 5. Each time, write the numeral on Diagram I and place the same number of straws on Diagram II. Make sure students see the relationship. Then when the numer is 5, replace the five ones with a bundle of five straws and place the bundle under the fives column. Write the number 5 on Diagram I. Indicate that five ones is the same as one bundle of five straws. Continue with the numerals 1, 2, 3, and 4 in the ones column, and make sure the students see that the new numbers are 11 = 6, 12 = 7, 13 = 8, and 14 = 9. Ask how many fives and ones the numbers 11, 12, 13, and 14 represent.

One hundred twenty-fives	Diagram I		
	Twenty-fives	Fives	Ones

One hundred twenty-fives	Diagram II		
	Twenty-fives	Fives	Ones

When five individual straws are in the ones column, the students should see that the five individual straws are again traded for another bundle of five straws that are placed in the fives column. Write the number 20 in Diagram I (with the 2 in the fives column and the 0 in the ones column). Discuss with the students the importance of the zero in the ones column. The zero indicates no straws are in the ones column. Discuss zero as a place holder. If students are experiencing difficulty, continue with the straws in Diagram II and the corresponding numerals in Diagram I.

You may write Diagram I on the board. Place Diagram II on the overhead.

Use the following Base Five numbers and discuss with students what the number is in Base Ten and where the number goes on Diagram I. Ask the students how they know the base for the numbers. Have students read each number as a Base Five number. Have the students determine that **4** is the largest number that will appear in the ones column in a base five system. Have the students indicate where five ones are recorded in a Base Five system. Use four bundles of fives and have the students see where five bundles of fives would be recorded. Place each of the numbers below on Diagram I.

1_5, 2_5, 3_5, 4_5, 10_5, 11_5, 12_5, 13_5, 14_5, 20_5, 21_5, 22_5, 23_5, 24_5, 30_5

Discuss with the students the value of each of the above numbers in Base Ten. Write the following on the overhead or board. Have students tell you what number each base and exponent represents. Write the number on the blank below each base and exponent. Then have the students tell you how many times greater the fives is than the ones, the twenty-fives than the fives, and the one hundred twenty-fives is than the twenty-fives. Write the answer on the second blank so students can see the answer.

	one hundred twenty-fives	twenty-fives	fives	ones
	5^3	5^2	5^1	5^0
Number:	_____	_____	_____	_____
Times greater:	_____	_____	_____	

Students need to learn how to find the value of a Base Five numeral in Base Ten. Teach the students using the following procedure. Write the following Base Five numbers on the overhead or board. 11_5, 23_5, 33_5, 44_5, 100_5 Remind students how to read Base Five numbers. Refer to Diagram I and discuss where the Base Five numbers should be placed on Diagram I. Place the Base Five numbers on Diagram I individually with a discussion of the value of the Base Five number in Base Ten.

Example: "11_5 is read as one-one Base Five. There is one five and one one. Five and one equals six in Base Ten." Continue with 23_5, 33_5, 44_5, and 100_5, using the same procedure. After introducing 11_5 and 23_5, students should take the lead in reading the number, placing the number on the chart, and interpreting the value in Base Ten.

125 + 300 = 42~~ 750 - 400 = 350   5 x (3 x 7) = 3 x (5 x 7)   3/4 - 1/4 = 1/2
5 x (3 x 7) = 3 x (5 x 7)   ~~ Understanding Addition~~25   750 - 400 = 350

Most middle school students have developed the basic mathematics skills needed for addition. However, it is important to determine when a middle school student has not mastered the math skills needed to be successful in addition.

Checking Understanding of Addition

Place the following problem on the board or overhead projector. Tell the students they are going to practice addition.

$$\begin{array}{r} 53 \\ + 23 \\ \hline \end{array}$$

Have the students perform the addition. Have the students verbalize the number in the ones column and then verbalize the number in the tens column.

Review what the numerals represent in the problem and then rewrite the problem on the board or overhead as

$$\begin{array}{r} 5 \text{ tens and } 3 \text{ ones} \\ + 2 \text{ tens and } 3 \text{ ones} \\ \hline \end{array}$$

Complete the addition with the students and write the answer as 7 tens and 6 ones.

Present the following problem on the board or overhead. Have the students tell you the steps that must be performed to solve the problem. Make certain students understand that ones, tens, and hundreds are being added.

$$\begin{array}{r} 54 \\ 454 \\ + 343 \\ \hline \text{sum} \end{array}$$

can students rewrite as 5 tens and 4 ones, add, and rewrite as 54?
can students rewrite as 4 hundreds 5 tens 4 ones, add, and rewrite as 454?
can students rewrite as 3 hundreds 4 tens 3 ones, add, and rewrite as 343?

Checking Skills in Regrouping

Regrouping poses a problem for many students because the students do not understand place value and have been taught regrouping as a mechanical procedure. The following exercise is designed to determine if students have mastered the regrouping skills needed to be successful in addition.

Place the following problem on the board or overhead projector. Tell the students they are going to practice addition. Have the students solve the problem below, which does not require regrouping.

53
+ 33   Have the students perform the addition. Have the students verbalize the number in the ones column and then the number in the tens column.

Next indicate that you are going to change the problem, and have students tell you how it is different before having the addition performed.

57
+ 33   Have the students perform the addition. Have the students verbalize the number in the ones column and then the number in the tens column.

Next indicate that you are going to change the problem again, and have students tell you how it is different before having the addition performed.

57
+ 64   Have the students perform the addition. Have the students verbalize the number in the ones column and then the number in the tens column.

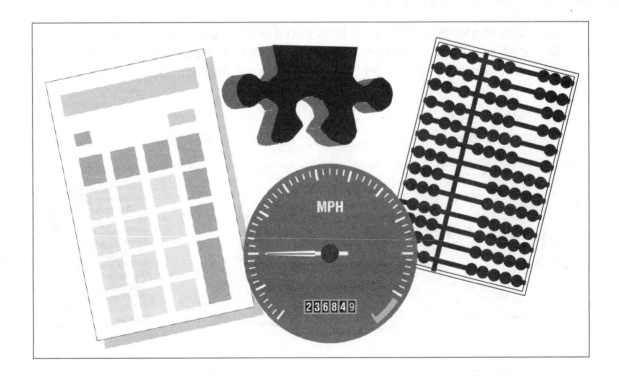

$125 + 300 = 42$ ~~750 - 400 = 350~~ $5 \times (3 \times 7) = 3 \times (5 \times 7)$ $3/4 - 1/4 = 1/2$

Understanding Subtraction

$5 \times (3 \times 7) = 3 \times (5 \times 7)$ ~~1/4 = 1/2~~ ~~125 + 300 = 425~~ $750 - 400 = 350$

Most middle school students have developed the basic mathematics skills needed for subtraction. However, today many middle school students have not mastered those skills. For many students, failure to master the basic subtraction facts and regrouping are two frequent causes of subtraction errors at the middle school level.

Checking Skills in Subtraction

Place the following problem on the board or overhead projector. Tell the students they are going to practice subtraction.

$$\begin{array}{r} 53 \\ -\ 22 \\ \hline \end{array}$$

Have the students perform the subtraction. Have the students verbalize the number in the ones column and then the number in the tens column.

Rewrite the problem on the board or overhead and have students solve the problem.

$$\begin{array}{r} 5 \text{ tens and } 3 \text{ ones} \\ -\ 2 \text{ tens and } 2 \text{ ones} \\ \hline \end{array}$$

Complete the subtraction with the students, and write the answer as 2 tens and 2 ones.

Present the following problems on the board or overhead one problem at a time. Have the students tell you the steps that must be performed to solve the problem. Make certain students can understand that ones, tens, and hundreds are being subtracted.

$$\begin{array}{r} 54 \\ -\ 45 \\ \hline \end{array}$$

can students rewrite as 5 tens and 4 ones, add, and rewrite as 54?
can students rewrite as 4 tens and 5 ones, add, and rewrite as 45?

$$\begin{array}{r} 454 \\ -\ 343 \\ \hline \end{array}$$

can students rewrite as 4 hundreds 5 tens 4 ones, add, and rewrite as 454
can students rewrite as 3 hundreds 4 tens 3 ones, add, and rewrite as 343

Checking Skills in Regouping

Regrouping poses a problem for many students because the students do not understand place value and have been taught regrouping as a mechanical procedure. The following exercise is designed to determine if students have mastered the regrouping skills needed to be successful in subtraction.

Place the following problem on the board or overhead projector. Tell the students they are going to practice subtraction. Have the students solve the problem below, which does not require regrouping.

53
- 31
———

Have the students perform the subtraction. Have the students verbalize the number in the ones column and then the number in the tens column. Write 2 tens and 2 ones on the overhead or board. Have students rewrite the answer as a number.

Next indicate that you are going to change the problem, and have students tell you how it is different before having the subtraction performed.

53
- 33
———

Have the students perform the subtraction. Have the students verbalize the number in the ones column and then the number in the tens column. Have students rewrite the answer as 2 tens and 0 ones. Discuss zero as place holder.

Next indicate that you are going to change the problem again, and have students tell you how it is different before having the subtraction performed.

53
- 34
———

Have the students verbalize the number in the ones column and then the number in the tens column. Have the students tell how this problem is different and what steps are required for subtracting. Have students rewrite the answer as 1 tens and 9 ones.

Next indicate that you are going to change the problem again, and have students tell you how it is different before having the subtraction performed.

253
- 164
———

Have the students perform the subtraction. Have the students verbalize the number in the ones column and then the number in the tens column and the number in the hundreds column.

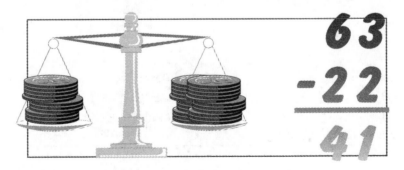

125 + 300 = 425   750 - 400 = 350   5 x (3 x 7) = 3 x (5 x 7)   3/4 - 1/4 = 1/2
5 x (3 x 7) = 3 x (5 x 7)   Understanding Multiplication   750 - 400 = 350

Teaching Multiplication Facts

Students need to have a memorized recall of the basic multiplication facts. Middle school students who have not accomplished a rote recall of the multiplication facts can benefit from the use of activities like the following.

a. Using flash cards with basic multiplication facts. The student is asked a multiplication fact and the student repeats the fact statement. The student then responds with an answer. The flash card is presented for verification. Once the student becomes proficient, the card is presented for two seconds or less, and the student responds with the answer.

b. Completion of fact charts like the following.

X	1	2	3	4	5	6	7	8	9	10
1										
2										
3										
4										
5										
6										
7										
8										
9										
10										

c. Use above completed chart, flash cards, and circular objects that can be placed over the numbers on the completed chart. Flash cards are presented individually, and students must as quickly as possible place a circular object over the answer on the completed chart. Students then verbalize the multiplication fact shown on the card.

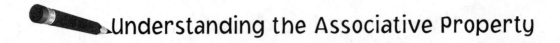

Understanding the Associative Property

Students need to understand and practice multiplication exercises using the **associative property of multiplication**. Present the following on the overhead or board. 2 x 3 x 5. Have the students multiply 2 x 3 then 6 x 5. Have the students multiply 3 x 5 and then 15 x 2. Use the following examples in the same manner. 5 x 7 x 3, 5 x 4 x 4, 6 x 5 x 8, and 9 x 2 x 5. Introduce the concept that numbers enclosed in parenthesis must be multiplied first.

Ask the students to solve the following:

(5 x 7) x 3 = (3 x 7) x 5 _____ = _____
5 x (4 x 4) = 4 x (4 x 5) _____ = _____
(6 x 5) x 8 = (8 x 5) x 6 _____ = _____
9 x (2 x 5) = 5 x (2 x 9) _____ = _____

Students must understand, that **the order of multiplication does not change the answer**. Once that is understood, use the following problems so students can see that by being selective, they can often simplify the multiplication process. Write 22 x 5 x 2 on the overhead or board. Have students multiply 22 x 5 then 110 x 2. Ask if there is a faster way to complete the multiplication. Students need to see that multiplying 2 x 5 then 10 x 22 is faster and less likely to produce errors. Continue with the following examples. Have students rearrange the problems into the order that is fastest and least likely to produce errors.

6 x 7 x 5 = _____   Suggested rearrangement _____ x _____ x _____ = _____
9 x 8 x 5 = _____   Suggested rearrangement _____ x _____ x _____ = _____
2 x 9 x 10 = _____   Suggested rearrangement _____ x _____ x _____ = _____

Have students solve the following. Have students talk about the steps used and encourage the students to use the order of multiplication that is most efficient.

23 x 5 x 2 = _____   56 x 2 x 10 = _____   43 x 10 x 5 = _____

Understanding the Distributive Property

Students need to understand and practice multiplication exercises using the **distributive property** of multiplication. Present 22 x 4 on the overhead or board. Discuss this as a multiplication problem. Work through the following first two examples with the students. Encourage questions/discussion with each step to ensure understanding. Place the third example on the overhead or board with blanks. Have students work to complete the blanks without teacher direction to check understanding.

4 x 22 =   88   3 x 33 =   99
4 (20 + 2) =   88   3 (30 + 3) =   99
4 x 20 + 4 x 2 = 80 + 8 = 88   3 x 30 + 3 x 3 = 90 + 9 = 99

5 x 41 = _____
5 x (_____ + _____) = _____
5 x _____ + 5 x _____ = _____

Developing Regrouping Skills

Students who have a command of the previous exercises are ready for regrouping. Present the example 15 + 15 + 15 on the overhead or board in **column form** and have students add the first column. How many ones? How many tens? You have 1 ten and 5 ones? Where do the ones go? Where does the 1 ten go? Complete the addition.

Now write 3 x 15 in column form. What does the sign (x) tell you to do? Multiply 3 x 5. How many ones? How many tens? You have 1 ten and 5 ones? Where do the 5 ones go? Where does the 1 ten go? Complete the multiplication with the students. Follow the same procedure with 6 x 14.

Write the following on the overhead or board in column form, and have students work through to check understanding.

5 x 16   3 x 28   2 x 20   4 x 19

Regrouping Using Two-Digit Numbers

Students who have a command of the above exercises are ready for two-digit regrouping. Present the example 26 x 45 on the overhead or board in **column form**. What does the sign (x) tell you to do? Have students multiply the first column. How many ones? How many tens? You have 3 tens and 0 ones? Where do you place the 0 ones? Where do you place the 3 tens? Complete the multiplication.

Next write in column form. What does the (x) tell you to do? Multiply 37 x 54. How many ones? How many tens? You have 2 tens and 8 ones? Where do the 8 ones go? Where do the 2 tens go? Complete the multiplication with the students. Follow the same procedure with 78 x 67.

Write each of the following on the overhead or board in column form, and have students work through to check understanding.

17 x 36   53 x 62   45 x 38

Regrouping Using Two- and Three-Digit Numbers

Students who have a command of two-digit regrouping are ready for regrouping using two- and three-digit numbers. Present the example 26 x 452 on the overhead or board in **column form**. What does the sign (x) tell you to do? Have students multiply the first column. How many ones? How many tens? You have 1 ten and 2 ones? Where do you place the ones? Where do you place the ten? Complete the multiplication.

Next write in column form. What does the sign (x) tell you to do? Multiply 375 x 54. Point to the ones column and have students perform the multiplication. How many ones? How many tens? You have 2 tens and 0 ones? Where does the 0 go? Where do the 2 tens go? Complete the multiplication with the students. Follow the same procedure with 787 x 67.

Write each of the following on the overhead or board in column form, and have students work through to check understanding.

17 x 362   53 x 625   45 x 284   345 x 456

$125 + 300 = 425$ $750 - 400 = 350$ $5 \times (3 \times 7) = 3 \times (5 \times 7)$ $3/4 - 1/4 = 1/2$
$5 \times (3 \times 7) = 3 \times (5 \times 7)$

Understanding Division

Many students in middle school are not proficient in division. The following exercises may be used for those students who need a review of division prior to assigning division activity sheets.

Checking Understanding of Division

Place the problems $\frac{12}{3}$ $3\overline{)12}$ and $12 \div 3$ on the overhead or board. Have students discuss the problems. Are the problems the same? What are you to find out to solve these problems? Who can solve the problems? How can the answer be checked? Continue until students can tell that the problem is to find out how many 3's are in 12. Show students that the answer could be found by repeated subtraction.

Example:

12	9	6	3	**four three's**
- 3	**- 3**	**- 3**	**- 3**	**in 12**
9	6	3	0	

Students must see that by repeated subtraction there are four 3's in 12. In division problems, the 12 is the **dividend**. Three is the **divisor**. The use of repeated subtraction is to emphasize that division is asking the students to find out how many of some number are found in another. It is not an efficient way to find the answer, however.

Place the following problems on the overhead or board. Have students tell you which number to circle as you say "dividend" or "divisor."

$4\overline{)16}$ $10 \div 2$ $20 \div 5$ $5\overline{)25}$

Place the following problems on the overhead or board one at a time. Have students work the problems under teacher direction. Ask students to identify the divisor and dividend. Ask the students what the problem is asking them to find.

$4\overline{)16}$ $3\overline{)12}$ $24 \div 6$ $4\overline{)24}$ $5\overline{)25}$

Break each problem down into step 1, 2, and 3 as shown below. Describe each step and have students verbalize the step aloud.

Step 1   Step 2   Step 3 (check answer)

$$4\overline{)16}^{\,4} \qquad 4\overline{)16}^{\,4} \atop \underline{16} \atop 0 \qquad 4 \times 4 = 16 \text{ Introduce the term "quotient" for an answer.}$$

Have students solve the following problems and check under teacher direction.

1. $3\overline{)9}$ 2. $5\overline{)15}$ 3. $4\overline{)20}$ 4. $8\overline{)24}$ 5. $9\overline{)36}$

Understanding Division and Remainders

Place the problems $3\overline{)13}$ and $13 \div 3$ on the overhead or board. Have students discuss the problems. Are the problems the same? What are you to find out to solve these problems? How many 3's are in 13? Once students arrive at 4, multiply $3 \times 4 = 12$. Write the 12 under the 13. Now tell students to subtract 12 from 13. What is the answer? So there are how many 3's in 13? How many are left over? Introduce the term **remainder**. How can the answer be checked? $3 \times 4 + 1 = 13$.

Place the following problems on the overhead or board. Have students tell you which number to circle as you say "dividend" or "divisor."

$4\overline{)18}$ $13 \div 2$ $23 \div 5$ $5\overline{)29}$

Have students work the problems under teacher direction. Ask students to identify the divisor and dividend. Ask the students what the problem is asking them to find. Have students identify the dividend, divisor, quotient, and remainder for each problem. Have students check the answer for each problem under teacher direction.

Break each problem down into step 1, 2, 3, and 4 as shown below. Describe each step and have students verbalize the step aloud.

Step 1	Step 2	Step 3	Step 4
$\dfrac{4}{4\overline{)18}}$	$4\overline{)18} \\ 16$	$4\ r2 \\ 4\overline{)18} \\ \underline{16} \\ 2$	$4 \times 4 + 2 = 18$

Have students solve the following problems and check under teacher direction.

1. $3\overline{)11}$ 2. $5\overline{)19}$ 3. $4\overline{)25}$ 4. $8\overline{)35}$ 5. $9\overline{)41}$

Division with Two-Digit Divisors Without Remainders

Place the problems $12\overline{)24}$ and $24 \div 12$ on the overhead or board. Have students discuss the problems. Are the problems the same? What are you to find out to solve these problems? How many 12's in 24? Once students arrive at 2, multiply 2 x 12 = 24. Write the 24 under the 24. Now tell students to subtract 24 from 24. What is the answer? So there are how many 12's in 24? How many are left over?

Place the following problems on the overhead or board. Have students solve each problem under teacher direction. Use the step procedure suggested in the previous exercises if needed to reinforce understanding. Have students check each problem.

1. $14\overline{)56}$ 2. $12\overline{)48}$ 3. $16\overline{)80}$ 4. $21\overline{)84}$ 5. $32\overline{)96}$

Have students complete the following problems under teacher direction. Have students work one problem at a time and check. The teacher then checks students' understanding before assigning the next problem.

1. $24\overline{)72}$ 2. $22\overline{)88}$ 3. $13\overline{)65}$ 4. $26\overline{)78}$ 5. $11\overline{)88}$

Use the same procedures as in the previous exercise with the following problems. Have students work through problems with teacher direction in a step-by-step procedure. Make students verbalize each step aloud. It is important that students express the reason for a step and the resulting answer. This ensures that the teacher can check for understanding of the division process.

1. $16\overline{)57}$ 2. $16\overline{)98}$

thirty-six divided by nine equals

125 + 300 = 42~~ 750 - 400 = 350   5 x (3 x 7) = 3 x (5 x 7)   3/4 - 1/4 = 1/2
5 x (3 x 7) = 3 x (5 x 7)   ~~/4 - 1/4 = 1/2   1~~ + ~~00 - ~~25   750 - 400 = 350

Understanding Fractions

Many middle school students do not understand fractions. Others can perform many of the operations with fractions but do not understand the ordering of fractions, the relationship of fractional parts to the whole, or the comparison of fractions.

The following fraction chart should be made available to students as they work with the fraction activities.

Fraction Chart

$\frac{1}{2}$	$\frac{2}{2}$

$\frac{1}{4}$	$\frac{2}{4}$	$\frac{3}{4}$	$\frac{4}{4}$

$\frac{1}{8}$	$\frac{2}{8}$	$\frac{3}{8}$	$\frac{4}{8}$	$\frac{5}{8}$	$\frac{6}{8}$	$\frac{7}{8}$	$\frac{8}{8}$

$\frac{1}{16}$	$\frac{2}{16}$	$\frac{3}{16}$	$\frac{4}{16}$	$\frac{5}{16}$	$\frac{6}{16}$	$\frac{7}{16}$	$\frac{8}{16}$	$\frac{9}{16}$	$\frac{10}{16}$	$\frac{11}{16}$	$\frac{12}{16}$	$\frac{13}{16}$	$\frac{14}{16}$	$\frac{15}{16}$	$\frac{16}{16}$

$\frac{1}{32}$	$\frac{2}{32}$	$\frac{3}{32}$	$\frac{4}{32}$	$\frac{5}{32}$	$\frac{6}{32}$	$\frac{7}{32}$	$\frac{8}{32}$	$\frac{9}{32}$	$\frac{10}{32}$	$\frac{11}{32}$	$\frac{12}{32}$	$\frac{13}{32}$	$\frac{14}{32}$	$\frac{15}{32}$	$\frac{16}{32}$	$\frac{17}{32}$	$\frac{18}{32}$	$\frac{19}{32}$	$\frac{20}{32}$	$\frac{21}{32}$	$\frac{22}{32}$	$\frac{23}{32}$	$\frac{24}{32}$	$\frac{25}{32}$	$\frac{26}{32}$	$\frac{27}{32}$	$\frac{28}{32}$	$\frac{29}{32}$	$\frac{30}{32}$	$\frac{31}{32}$	$\frac{32}{32}$

Understanding Simple Fractions

Place the above fraction chart on the board or overhead and explain it is a Fraction Chart. Introduce the concept of simple fractions. The fractions on the Fraction Chart are simple fractions.

Write the following fractions on the overhead or board. $\frac{1}{2}$ $\frac{1}{4}$ $\frac{1}{8}$ $\frac{1}{16}$ $\frac{1}{32}$ Discuss the characteristics that make these **simple fractions**. Each has a **numerator** and **denominator**. Make sure students can identify the numerator and denominator. Students must understand that the denominator (bottom number) tells how many total parts. The numerator (top number) tells how many parts are being identified.

Place a fraction strip like the following on the overhead or board. Write the fraction $\frac{1}{4}$ on the overhead or board. Have the strip divided into fourths. Have one of the fourths shaded.

Point out that the denominator of $\frac{1}{4}$ tells there are four equal parts in the strip. The numerator for $\frac{1}{4}$ is shaded and tells how many parts are identified. One of the four parts.

$\frac{1}{4}$	$\frac{2}{4}$	$\frac{3}{4}$	$\frac{4}{4}$

Place the following fraction strip on the board or overhead. Have the strip marked into sixteen equal parts. Make the same fraction strips available for students.

$\frac{1}{16}$	$\frac{2}{16}$	$\frac{3}{16}$	$\frac{4}{16}$	$\frac{5}{16}$	$\frac{6}{16}$	$\frac{7}{16}$	$\frac{8}{16}$	$\frac{9}{16}$	$\frac{10}{16}$	$\frac{11}{16}$	$\frac{12}{16}$	$\frac{13}{16}$	$\frac{14}{16}$	$\frac{15}{16}$	$\frac{16}{16}$

Step 1: Have students fold the strip into two equal halves. Unfold the strip and write $\frac{1}{2}$ on the overhead strip. Have students do the same on their strips.

Step 2: Have students fold a second fraction strip into two equal halves and then fold again into two equal halves. Unfold the strip and write $\frac{1}{4}$, $\frac{2}{4}$, $\frac{3}{4}$, and $\frac{4}{4}$ on the overhead strip. Have students do the same on their strips. Have students compare the strips. Call attention to the fact that $\frac{8}{16}$ and $\frac{2}{4}$ both divide the fraction strips in half.

Questions:

The first strip is divided into how many equal parts? Each part is what part of the total? The second strip is divided into how many equal parts? Each part is what part of the total? How many fourths equal $\frac{1}{2}$?

Continue the above with strips for $\frac{1}{8}$'s, $\frac{1}{16}$'s, and $\frac{1}{32}$'s. Continue with questions that call attention to the equivalence of various fractions. Call attention to the fact that the larger the denominator, the smaller the fraction. Make copies of the fraction table for students to use as they study simple fractions.

The following strips are divided into fourths, eighths, and sixteenths. Have students color $\frac{1}{4}$, $\frac{1}{8}$, and $\frac{1}{16}$. Compare the size of these fractions. Have the students understand that the larger the denominator, the smaller the fraction.

$\frac{1}{4}$	$\frac{2}{4}$	$\frac{3}{4}$	$\frac{4}{4}$

$\frac{1}{8}$	$\frac{2}{8}$	$\frac{3}{8}$	$\frac{4}{8}$	$\frac{5}{8}$	$\frac{6}{8}$	$\frac{7}{8}$	$\frac{8}{8}$

$\frac{1}{16}$	$\frac{2}{16}$	$\frac{3}{16}$	$\frac{4}{16}$	$\frac{5}{16}$	$\frac{6}{16}$	$\frac{7}{16}$	$\frac{8}{16}$	$\frac{9}{16}$	$\frac{10}{16}$	$\frac{11}{16}$	$\frac{12}{16}$	$\frac{13}{16}$	$\frac{14}{16}$	$\frac{15}{16}$	$\frac{16}{16}$

Have students refer to the strips and determine that $\frac{1}{4}$ equals $\frac{4}{16}$ and $\frac{1}{8} = \frac{2}{16}$. Place the following on the overhead or board.

A		B
$\frac{1}{16}$	$=$	$\frac{1}{16}$
$\frac{1}{8}$	$=$	$\frac{2}{16}$
$\frac{1}{4}$	$=$	$\frac{4}{16}$

Have students read the fractions in Column A. Locate the fractions on the strips. What does the denominator tell you in each fraction? What does the numerator tell you? Have students read the fractions in Column B. What does the denominator tell you? What does the numerator tell you? How are the fractions alike? Ask the students which fraction is largest? Smallest? How can they tell?

Introduce that the fractions in Column B have been changed to fractions with a **common denominator**. Have students see that the distance on the strips measured by $\frac{1}{8}$ and $\frac{2}{16}$ is the same. The distance on the strips measured by $\frac{1}{4}$ and $\frac{4}{16}$ is the same. The only thing changed is the denominators.

Write $\frac{2}{4}$ and $\frac{4}{8}$ on the overhead or board. Have students refer to the strips and tell how many sixteenths each fraction equals. Do the same for $\frac{3}{4}$ and $\frac{6}{8}$.

Place the Fractions Chart on the overhead and place copies in students hands. Tell students they will be finding the common denominators for certain fractions. Have students answer the following with close teacher direction.

1. $\frac{1}{4} = \frac{}{8}$ 2. $\frac{1}{2} = \frac{}{8}$ 3. $\frac{8}{16} = \frac{}{8}$ 4. $\frac{3}{4} = \frac{}{8}$

5. $\frac{1}{8} = \frac{}{16}$ 6. $\frac{6}{16} = \frac{}{8}$ 7. $\frac{7}{8} = \frac{}{16}$ 8. $\frac{1}{2} = \frac{}{4}$

Discuss **equivalent** fractions and fractions with a **common denominator**. Have students change each of the following fractions to an **equivalent** fraction with a **common denominator**.

1. $\frac{2}{8} = \frac{}{16}$ 2. $\frac{2}{4} = \frac{}{16}$ 3. $\frac{3}{4} = \frac{}{16}$ 4. $\frac{1}{2} = \frac{}{16}$

 Changing Fractions to Equivalent Fractions

Write the fractions $\frac{1}{2}$, $\frac{1}{4}$, and $\frac{1}{8}$ on the overhead or board.

Have students refer to the fraction chart and determine how many fourths equal one-half. Have students determine how many eighths equal one-fourth. Have students determine how many sixteenths equal one-eighth. Write the fraction $\frac{1}{2}$ on the overhead. Have students identify the numerator and denominator. Place $\frac{1}{2}$ x $\frac{2}{2}$ = — on the board or overhead. Demonstrate fraction multiplication, calling attention to the fact that it is necessary to multiply numerators and denominators. Write the fraction $\frac{2}{4}$ in the blank. Ask the students. "How many fourths does one-half equal?" Now write $\frac{1}{2}$ x $\frac{4}{4}$ = — on the overhead or board. Complete the multiplication. Ask the students the name of the new fraction.

Ask students to look at the fraction table and tell how many eighths equals one-half. Complete the same steps with $\frac{1}{2}$ x $\frac{8}{8}$ = —.

Review with students that in each case the numerator and denominator were multiplied by the same number to get an equivalent fraction to one-half. Have students complete the following problems under teacher direction.

$\frac{1}{2}$ x $\frac{3}{3}$ = — $\frac{1}{4}$ x $\frac{2}{2}$ = — $\frac{1}{3}$ x $\frac{3}{3}$ = — $\frac{1}{5}$ x $\frac{4}{4}$ = —

Discuss with students why the above are equivalent fractions. Have students complete the following problems.

1. $\frac{1}{2}$ x $\frac{4}{4}$ = —   3. $\frac{1}{8}$ x $\frac{3}{3}$ = —   5. $\frac{1}{6}$ x $\frac{2}{2}$ = —

2. $\frac{1}{3}$ x $\frac{4}{4}$ = —   4. $\frac{1}{5}$ x $\frac{4}{4}$ = —   6. $\frac{1}{10}$ x $\frac{2}{2}$ = —

More About Changing Fracions to Equivalent Fractions

Repeat the same procedure as above, using simple fractions with numerators other than 1.

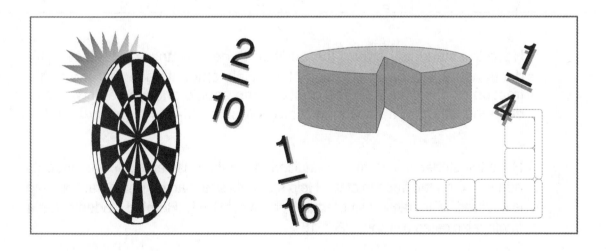

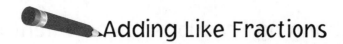

Adding Like Fractions

Place the following on the overhead or board. Tell students they are going to add fractions. Discuss how the fractions are alike and different. Have students tell how the numerators are different. Discuss how the denominators are alike. Help students determine that these are **simple fractions** with **common denominators**. Have students tell why the fractions are simple and what it means to have a common denominator. Have students add the numerators. Write the answer below the problem.

$$\frac{1}{4} + \frac{2}{4} = \frac{1}{4}$$
$$+ \frac{2}{4}$$

Next present the following simple fractions with common denominators. Have students determine the answers with teacher direction.

$$\frac{3}{8} \qquad\qquad \frac{2}{6}$$
$$+ \frac{1}{8} \qquad\qquad + \frac{3}{6}$$

Present the following problems for the students to solve. Have students write the problems in column form.

1. $\frac{1}{8}$ 2. $\frac{1}{6}$ 3. $\frac{2}{7}$ 4. $\frac{5}{8}$
   $+ \frac{2}{8}$ $+ \frac{3}{6}$ $+ \frac{3}{7}$ $+ \frac{2}{8}$

Next present the following simple fractions with common denominators. Have students determine the answers with teacher direction. Have fraction strips, such as these below, available for students.

$\frac{1}{8}$	$\frac{2}{8}$	$\frac{3}{8}$	$\frac{4}{8}$	$\frac{5}{8}$	$\frac{6}{8}$	$\frac{7}{8}$	$\frac{8}{8}$

$\frac{1}{16}$	$\frac{2}{16}$	$\frac{3}{16}$	$\frac{4}{16}$	$\frac{5}{16}$	$\frac{6}{16}$	$\frac{7}{16}$	$\frac{8}{16}$	$\frac{9}{16}$	$\frac{10}{16}$	$\frac{11}{16}$	$\frac{12}{16}$	$\frac{13}{16}$	$\frac{14}{16}$	$\frac{15}{16}$	$\frac{16}{16}$

$\frac{1}{3}$	$\frac{2}{3}$	$\frac{3}{3}$

$\frac{5}{8}$
$+ \frac{3}{8}$
$\frac{8}{8}$

Have the students perform the addition to get the answer $\frac{8}{8}$. Have students add $\frac{5}{8} + \frac{3}{8}$ on the fraction strip. Help students see that the entire fraction strip is covered. The fraction strip equals one whole or 1. Introduce the idea that a fraction indicates division. $8 \div 8 = 1$ or $8\overline{)8} = 1$.

$\frac{9}{16}$
$+ \frac{7}{16}$
$\frac{16}{16}$

Have the students perform the addition to get the answer $\frac{16}{16}$. Have students add $\frac{9}{16} + \frac{7}{16}$ on the fraction strip. Help students see that the entire fraction strip is covered. The fraction strip equals one whole or 1. Remind students that a fraction indicates division. $16 \div 16 = 1$.

Have students add $\frac{1}{3} + \frac{2}{3}$ and complete as above. Have students complete the division exercise.

Have students solve the following problems with teacher direction. Have students complete the division exercise to show each addition equals one.

1. $\frac{1}{2}$
   $+ \frac{1}{2}$

2. $\frac{3}{4}$
   $+ \frac{1}{4}$

3. $\frac{4}{7}$
   $+ \frac{3}{7}$

4. $\frac{3}{8}$
   $+ \frac{5}{8}$

5. $\frac{21}{32}$
   $+ \frac{11}{32}$

6. $\frac{5}{12}$
   $+ \frac{7}{12}$

7. $\frac{3}{24}$
   $+ \frac{21}{24}$

8. $\frac{2}{5}$
   $+ \frac{3}{5}$

Adding Unlike Fractions

Place $\frac{1}{2}$ and $\frac{2}{4}$ on the overhead or board. Tell students they are going to add fractions with unlike numerators and denominators. Discuss how the fractions are alike and different. Have students tell how the numerators are different and the denominators are different. Help students determine that these are simple fractions with unlike denominators. Have students tell why the fractions are simple and what it means to have an unlike denominator. Discuss with students how to change the fractions so that both fractions have a common denominator. Refer to the Fraction Chart, if needed. Otherwise, move immediately to converting $\frac{1}{2}$ to $\frac{2}{4}$. Place the following on the overhead or board. $\frac{1}{2} \times \frac{2}{2} = $ —. Have students solve.

Place the following on the overhead or board. Have students add the numerators. Write the answer below the problem.

<u>Problem/Unlike Denominators/Common Denominators</u>

$\frac{1}{4} + \frac{1}{2} = $ $\frac{1}{4}$ $ = \frac{1}{4}$

                    $+\frac{1}{2}$ $ = +\frac{2}{4}$

                    Answer =

Next present the following simple fractions with unlike denominators. Have students change to common denominators with teacher direction. Then have them determine the answers with teacher direction.

$\frac{3}{8} = \frac{3}{8}$ $\frac{1}{3} = \frac{}{6}$

$+\frac{1}{2} = \frac{}{8}$ $+\frac{3}{6} = \frac{3}{6}$

Present the following problems for the students to solve.

1. $\frac{1}{2}$
   $+ \frac{2}{8}$

2. $\frac{1}{6}$
   $+ \frac{2}{3}$

3. $\frac{1}{2}$
   $+ \frac{2}{4}$

4. $\frac{5}{16}$
   $+ \frac{2}{8}$

Improper Fractions

Write the following on the overhead or board. $\frac{1}{2}$ $\frac{2}{2}$ $\frac{3}{2}$. Place the fraction lines below on the overhead or board.

A.

$\frac{1}{2}$ = $\frac{1}{2}$

B.

$\frac{1}{2}$ + $\frac{1}{2}$ = $\frac{2}{2}$ = 1

C.

$\frac{1}{2}$ + $\frac{1}{2}$ + $\frac{1}{2}$ = $\frac{3}{2}$ = $1\frac{1}{2}$

Point out to the students that fraction line "A" equals $\frac{1}{2}$. Point out that the numerator is smaller than the denominator. $\frac{1}{2}$ is a simple fraction. Point out to the students that fraction line "B" is exactly two times the length of fraction line "A." Point out that the numerator and denominator are exactly the same. Two halves $\frac{2}{2}$ = 1. Complete the division 2 ÷ 2 = 1. Point out that fraction line "C" is three halves. Since two halves equal one, three halves is $1 + \frac{1}{2}$ or $\frac{3}{2}$.

Point out that $\frac{1}{2}$ is a **simple fraction** with the numerator smaller than the denominator. Point out that $\frac{3}{2}$ is called an **improper fraction** because the numerator is larger than the denominator.

Write the following simple and improper fractions on the overhead or board. Have the students indicate if the fraction is simple or improper as you point to each fraction. Have students tell why the fraction is simple or improper.

$\frac{1}{2}$ $\frac{3}{2}$ $\frac{3}{4}$ $\frac{4}{3}$ $\frac{2}{5}$ $\frac{2}{3}$ $\frac{6}{5}$ $\frac{8}{7}$ $\frac{1}{3}$ $\frac{10}{11}$ $\frac{12}{10}$

Next have the students tell which of the above fractions is more or less than one. Have students indicate **simple** or **improper** and **more** or **less** than one.

Next write the following improper fraction on the overhead or board. $\frac{3}{2}$ Remind students that this is an improper fraction. Have students tell why the fraction is improper. Introduce again that a number written as a fraction indicates division. Have students verbalize 3 divided by 2.

The improper fraction $\frac{3}{2}$ = $2\overline{)3}$ $\begin{array}{r} 1 \\ 2\overline{)3} \\ \underline{2} \\ \frac{1}{2} \end{array}$ = $1\frac{1}{2}$

Point out that the **improper fraction** $\frac{3}{2}$ = $1\frac{1}{2}$ a **mixed number**. **A mixed number is a whole number and fraction.**

Have students change each of the following improper fractions to a mixed number. Check each one before having students complete the next problem.

$\frac{4}{3}$ $\frac{6}{5}$ $\frac{8}{7}$ $\frac{12}{10}$

Have students change the following improper fractions to mixed numbers.

1. $\frac{6}{5}$ 2. $\frac{4}{3}$ 3. $\frac{8}{7}$ 4. $\frac{12}{11}$ 5. $\frac{5}{4}$

Write the following improper fraction on the overhead or board. $\frac{25}{8}$. Have students complete the division to get the quotient $3\frac{1}{8}$.

Point out that $\frac{25}{8} = \frac{8}{8} + \frac{8}{8} + \frac{8}{8} + \frac{1}{8}$ or $3\frac{1}{8}$

$\frac{25}{8} = 1 + 1 + 1 + \frac{1}{8}$ or $3\frac{1}{8}$ Discuss why $\frac{8}{8} = 1$

Place the following on the overhead or board. Have students change the following improper fractions to a mixed number.

$\frac{8}{3} = - + - + - = \_\_ -$

$\frac{8}{3} = \_\_ + \_\_ + - = \_\_ -$

Have students change the following improper fractions to mixed numbers.

1. $\frac{5}{4}$ 2. $\frac{3}{2}$ 3. $\frac{8}{5}$ 4. $\frac{11}{9}$ 5. $\frac{17}{16}$ 6. $\frac{4}{3}$

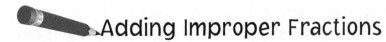

Adding Improper Fractions

Place the following improper fractions on the overhead or board. Tell students they are going to learn to add improper fractions.

Step 1: $\frac{5}{3} + \frac{4}{3}$ or $\begin{array}{r} \frac{5}{3} \\ + \frac{4}{3} \\ \hline \frac{9}{3} \end{array}$ The denominators are both the same. So simply add the numerators. Next, change to a whole or mixed number.

$9 \div 3 = \frac{9}{3} = 3$

Step 2: Place the following on the overhead or board.

$\frac{9}{3} = \frac{3}{3} + \frac{3}{3} + \frac{3}{3} = 3$ $\frac{9}{3} = 1 + 1 + 1 = 3$

Place the following problem on the overhead or board and have the students solve.

$\frac{3}{2} + \frac{6}{2}$ or $\begin{array}{r} \frac{3}{2} \\ + \frac{6}{2} \\ \hline \end{array}$ Have students complete Step 1 and 2.

Have students complete the following problems using Steps 1 and 2. Students should change each answer to a whole number or mixed number.

1. $\begin{array}{r} \frac{5}{4} \\ + \frac{6}{4} \\ \hline \end{array}$ 2. $\begin{array}{r} \frac{6}{5} \\ + \frac{7}{5} \\ \hline \end{array}$ 3. $\begin{array}{r} \frac{8}{6} \\ + \frac{1}{6} \\ \hline \end{array}$ 4. $\begin{array}{r} \frac{9}{7} \\ + \frac{8}{7} \\ \hline \end{array}$ 5. $\begin{array}{r} \frac{13}{12} \\ + \frac{15}{12} \\ \hline \end{array}$

Adding Improper Fractions with Unlike Denominators

Place the following on the overhead or board. Tell students they are going to learn to add improper fractions with unlike denominators.

Step 1:

$\frac{5}{4} + \frac{4}{3}$ or $\frac{5}{4}$
$+ \frac{4}{3}$

The denominators are unlike so they must be changed to equivalent denominators. Multiply $\frac{5}{4} \times \frac{3}{3}$ and $\frac{4}{3} \times \frac{4}{4}$

$\frac{5}{4} \times \frac{3}{3} = \frac{15}{12}$
$\frac{4}{3} \times \frac{4}{4} = \frac{16}{12}$

Now place in column form and add.

$\frac{15}{12}$
$+ \frac{16}{12}$
$\frac{31}{12} = 2\frac{7}{12}$

Add the numerators.
Complete division $\frac{31}{12} = 31 \div 12 = 2\frac{7}{12}$

Step 2:
Place the following on the overhead or board.

$\frac{31}{12} = \frac{12}{12} + \frac{12}{12} + \frac{7}{12} = 2\frac{7}{12}$
$\frac{31}{12} = 1 + 1 + \frac{7}{12} = 2\frac{7}{12}$

Place the following problem on the overhead or board and have the students solve.

$\frac{6}{3} + \frac{3}{2}$ or $\frac{6}{3}$
$+ \frac{3}{2}$

Have students complete Steps 1 and 2 from above.

Have students complete the following problems using Steps 1 and 2.

1. $\frac{5}{4}$
$+ \frac{6}{3}$

2. $\frac{6}{5}$
$+ \frac{3}{2}$

3. $\frac{8}{6}$
$+ \frac{1}{2}$

4. $\frac{9}{3}$
$+ \frac{8}{5}$

5. $\frac{8}{3}$
$+ \frac{7}{5}$

Subtracting Fractions

Place the following on the overhead or board. Tell students they are going to subtract fractions.

A. 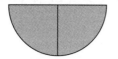   B.

Shade in two of the $\frac{1}{4}$ parts of A. If one of the two shaded $\frac{1}{4}$ parts is taken away you have one of the shaded $\frac{1}{4}$ parts left, as shown in B.

42

Place the following problem on the overhead or board. Discuss how the fractions are alike and different. Have students tell how the numerators are different and how the denominators are alike. Help students determine that these are **simple fractions** with **common denominators**. Have students tell why the fractions are simple and what it means to have a common denominator. Have students subtract the numerators.

$$\frac{2}{4} - \frac{1}{4} \text{ or } \begin{array}{r} \frac{2}{4} \\ -\frac{1}{4} \\ \hline \frac{1}{4} \end{array}$$

Present two circles divided into eighths and sixths. Shade $\frac{3}{8}$ on one circle and $\frac{3}{6}$ on the other. If needed, have students remove one of the shaded eighths and tell how many shaded eights are left. Do the same with the sixths. Next present the following simple fractions with common denominators. Have students determine the answers with teacher direction.

$$\begin{array}{r} \frac{3}{8} \\ -\frac{1}{8} \\ \hline \end{array}$$  $$\begin{array}{r} \frac{3}{6} \\ -\frac{2}{6} \\ \hline \end{array}$$

Present the following problems for the students to solve.

1. $\begin{array}{r} \frac{5}{8} \\ -\frac{2}{8} \\ \hline \end{array}$ 2. $\begin{array}{r} \frac{3}{6} \\ -\frac{1}{6} \\ \hline \end{array}$ 3. $\begin{array}{r} \frac{5}{7} \\ -\frac{3}{7} \\ \hline \end{array}$ 4. $\begin{array}{r} \frac{5}{10} \\ -\frac{2}{10} \\ \hline \end{array}$

5. $\begin{array}{r} \frac{21}{32} \\ -\frac{11}{32} \\ \hline \end{array}$ 6. $\begin{array}{r} \frac{7}{12} \\ -\frac{5}{12} \\ \hline \end{array}$ 7. $\begin{array}{r} \frac{23}{24} \\ -\frac{21}{24} \\ \hline \end{array}$ 8. $\begin{array}{r} \frac{4}{5} \\ -\frac{1}{5} \\ \hline \end{array}$

Subtracting Unlike Fractions

Place $\frac{1}{2}$ and $\frac{2}{4}$ on the overhead or board. Tell the students they are going to subtract fractions with unlike numerators and denominators. Discuss how the fractions are alike and different. Have students tell how the numerators are different and how the denominators are different. Help students determine that these are simple fractions with unlike denominators. Have students tell why the fractions are simple and what it means to have an unlike denominator. Discuss with students how to change the fractions so that both fractions have a common denominator. Refer to the Fraction Chart, if needed. Otherwise move immediately to converting $\frac{1}{2}$ to $\frac{2}{4}$. Place the following on the overhead or board. $\frac{1}{2} \times \frac{2}{2} = —$. Have students solve.

Place the following on the overhead or board. Have students subtract the numerators. Write the answer below the problem.

<u>Problem/Unlike Denominators/Common Denominators</u>

$$\begin{array}{cccc} \frac{1}{2} - \frac{1}{4} = & \begin{array}{r} \frac{1}{2} \\ -\frac{1}{4} \\ \hline \end{array} & \frac{1}{2} \times \frac{2}{2} & \begin{array}{r} = \frac{2}{4} \\ = -\frac{1}{4} \\ \hline \end{array} \end{array}$$

Answer =

Next present the following simple fractions with unlike denominators. Have students change them to common denominators with teacher direction. Then have them determine the answers with teacher direction.

$$\frac{3}{8} = \frac{3}{8}$$
$$-\frac{1}{4} = \frac{}{8}$$

$$\frac{3}{6} = \frac{3}{6}$$
$$-\frac{1}{3} = \frac{}{6}$$

Present the following problems for the students to solve.

1. $\frac{1}{2}$
   $-\frac{2}{8}$

2. $\frac{2}{3}$
   $-\frac{1}{6}$

3. $\frac{3}{4}$
   $-\frac{1}{2}$

4. $\frac{9}{16}$
   $-\frac{2}{8}$

Subtracting Improper Fractions With Unlike Denominators

Place the following improper fractions on the overhead or board. Tell students they are going to learn to subtract improper fractions.

Step 1:

$\frac{4}{3} - \frac{5}{4}$ or $\frac{4}{3}$ Multiply to get fraction with common denominator. Subtract the numerators.
$\qquad\qquad -\frac{5}{3}$ $\frac{4}{3} \times \frac{4}{4} = \frac{16}{12}$ and $\frac{5}{4} \times \frac{3}{3} = \frac{15}{12}$ $\frac{16}{12}$
$\qquad\qquad\qquad\qquad\qquad\qquad\qquad\qquad\qquad\qquad\qquad\qquad\qquad -\frac{15}{12}$
$\qquad\qquad\qquad\qquad\qquad\qquad\qquad\qquad\qquad\qquad\qquad\qquad\qquad \frac{1}{12}$

Place the following problem on the overhead or board and have the students solve.

$\frac{6}{3} - \frac{3}{2}$ or $\frac{6}{3} = \frac{6}{3} \times \frac{2}{2} = \frac{}{}$
$\qquad\qquad -\frac{3}{2} = -\frac{3}{2} \times \frac{3}{3} = -\frac{}{}$

Have students complete the following problems.

1. $\frac{6}{3} - \frac{5}{4} = \frac{6}{3} = \frac{6}{3} \times \frac{4}{4} = \frac{}{}$
   $\qquad\qquad\qquad -\frac{5}{4} = \frac{5}{4} \times \frac{3}{3} = -\frac{}{}$

2. $\frac{6}{5} - \frac{1}{2} = \frac{6}{5} = \frac{6}{5} \times \frac{2}{2} = \frac{}{}$
   $\qquad\qquad\qquad -\frac{1}{2} = \frac{1}{2} \times \frac{5}{5} = -\frac{}{}$

3. $\frac{8}{5} - \frac{8}{6} = \frac{8}{5} = \frac{8}{5} \times \frac{6}{6} = \frac{}{}$
   $\qquad\qquad\qquad -\frac{8}{6} = \frac{8}{6} \times \frac{5}{5} = -\frac{}{}$

4. $\frac{9}{3} - \frac{7}{4} = \frac{9}{3} = \frac{9}{3} \times \frac{}{} = \frac{}{}$
   $\qquad\qquad\qquad -\frac{7}{4} = \frac{7}{4} \times \frac{}{} = -\frac{}{}$

5. $\frac{8}{3} - \frac{3}{2} = \frac{8}{3} = \frac{8}{3} \times \frac{}{} = \frac{}{}$
   $\qquad\qquad\qquad -\frac{3}{2} = \frac{3}{2} \times \frac{}{} = -\frac{}{}$

Multiplication of Fractions

Students have learned that multiplication of whole numbers produces an answer that is equal to or larger than either of the numbers multiplied. Students have also learned that multiplication is a short form of addition. When teaching students to multiply fractions, it is important that students understand that when fractions are multiplied, the answer is a smaller fraction. Students must understand that multiplication of fractions is not always a short form of addition.

Multiplication of fractions includes multiplying a whole number times a fraction, a fraction times a whole number, a fraction times a fraction, and a mixed number times a mixed number. The fraction activity pages will include these four multiplication activities with fractions.

Multiplying Whole Numbers Times a Fraction

Present the following on the overhead or board. Tell students they are going to learn to multiply whole numbers and fractions.

Whole Numbers are 0, 1, 2, 3, 4, 5, 6, 7, 8, and 9. Explain to students that these are called whole numbers.

Fractions include numbers like $\frac{1}{2}$ and $\frac{3}{4}$. Have students give example of other fractions.

Mixed Numbers include numbers like $1\frac{1}{2}$ and $1\frac{3}{4}$. Have students give examples of other mixed numbers.

Place the following on the overhead or board. $4 \times \frac{3}{4}$

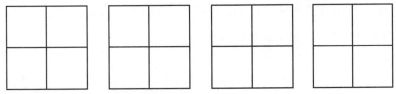

Indicate to students that the problem $4 \times \frac{3}{4}$ is asking for 4 groups of $\frac{3}{4}$ each. Shade in $\frac{3}{4}$ of each of the above squares. Then show students that the problem is asking for four groups of $\frac{3}{4}$. $\frac{3}{4} + \frac{3}{4} + \frac{3}{4} + \frac{3}{4} = \frac{12}{4} = 3$, or $4 \times \frac{3}{4} = \frac{4}{1} \times \frac{3}{4} = \frac{12}{4} = 4\overline{)12} = 3$.

Place $4 \times \frac{2}{3}$ on the overhead or board. Tell students this problem is asking for four groups of $\frac{2}{3}$. $\frac{2}{3} + \frac{2}{3} + \frac{2}{3} + \frac{2}{3} = \frac{8}{3} = 2\frac{2}{3}$, or $4 \times \frac{2}{3} = \frac{4}{1} \times \frac{2}{3} = \frac{8}{3} = 3\overline{)8} = 2\frac{2}{3}$

Place the problem $5 \times \frac{1}{2}$ on the overhead or board. Have students solve the problem. Check for understanding and assign the problems below. Work problem #1 with students. Have students complete the remaining problems using the same format as #1.

1. $3 \times \frac{2}{3} = $ __ + __ + __ = __

   $3 \times \frac{2}{3} = \frac{3}{1} \times \frac{2}{3} = $ ___ $= \overline{)}$ ___ $= $ ___

2. $4 \times \frac{1}{5} = \frac{4}{1} \times \frac{1}{5} = $

3. $5 \times \frac{2}{3} = $

4. $2 \times \frac{3}{5} = $

Multiplication of Fractions by a Whole number

In these problems the student is finding the fraction part of a whole. For example, $\frac{2}{3}$ of a dozen oranges is how many oranges? Place the following problem on the overhead or board.

$\frac{2}{3}$ x 12

$\frac{2}{3}$ of a dozen oranges. (Make sure students know the number of oranges in a dozen). Draw 12 small circles for oranges on the overhead or board. Circle groups of four and write $\frac{1}{3}$ under each circled group. $\frac{1}{3} + \frac{1}{3} + \frac{1}{3} = \frac{3}{3} = 1$ dozen oranges. Have students count the number of oranges in $\frac{2}{3}$. Write $\frac{2}{3}$ x 12 = 8 oranges. Then write the following on the overhead or board and demonstrate the solution.

$\frac{2}{3}$ x 12 = $\frac{2}{3}$ x $\frac{12}{1}$ = $\frac{24}{3}$ = 8 oranges.

Place the following on the board or overhead and have students solve. $\frac{3}{4}$ of 12 oranges = $\frac{3}{4}$ x 12. Place 12 small circles on the overhead or board and discuss what the denominator 4 tells us about the number of groups of oranges that should be circled. Then ask how many should be in each group. Circle the four groups of three oranges. Have students tell how many fourths each group of three oranges equals ($\frac{1}{4}$). Have students determine the number of oranges in $\frac{3}{4}$.

$\frac{1}{4} + \frac{1}{4} + \frac{1}{4} = \frac{3}{4}$

3 + 3 + 3 = 9 oranges

Show students $\frac{3}{4}$ x 12 = $\frac{3}{4}$ x $\frac{12}{1}$ = $\frac{36}{4}$ = $4\overline{)36}^{\,9}$

Have students solve the problem $\frac{2}{3}$ x 9 using the above format.

Assign the following problems for students to solve.

1. $\frac{2}{3}$ x 15

2. $\frac{3}{4}$ x 8

3. $\frac{2}{5}$ x 5

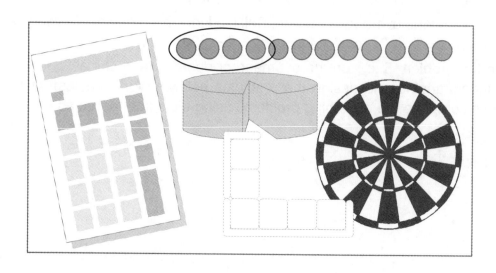

Multiplication of Fraction by Fraction

Students must understand that multiplication of fractions results in a fraction smaller than either of the two fractions multiplied. Place the rectangle below divided in halves and fourths on the overhead or board.

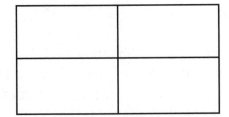

Shade in $\frac{1}{2}$ and discuss that $\frac{1}{2}$ of the rectangle has been shaded. Then haschure (/////) $\frac{1}{4}$ of the rectangle. Have students compare the $\frac{1}{2}$ and $\frac{1}{4}$ area of the rectangle.

Write the following problem on the overhead or board. $\frac{1}{2}$ x $\frac{1}{4}$. Teach students that multiplication of two fractions is completed by multiplying numerators and multiplying denominators. $\underline{1 \times 1 = 1}$

$2 \times 4 = 8 = \frac{1}{8}$

Place the below rectangle on the overhead or board. Divide the rectangle into eighths. Make sure the rectangle is the same size as the one used above.

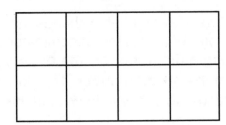

Show the problem $\frac{1}{2}$ x $\frac{1}{4} = \frac{1}{8}$. Shade in $\frac{1}{8}$ on the rectangle. Then show students that $\frac{1}{4}$ and $\frac{1}{2}$ both cover a larger area than does $\frac{1}{8}$, the answer when $\frac{1}{2}$ x $\frac{1}{4}$ is multiplied.

Place the following rectangle on the overhead or board. Have students shade in $\frac{1}{3}$. Haschure in $\frac{1}{2}$.

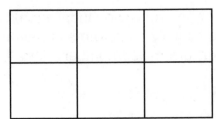

Have students solve $\frac{1}{3}$ x $\frac{1}{2}$. Have students shade in the answer $\frac{1}{6}$ on the rectangle. Discuss the area of each. Emphasize the smaller area following multiplication.

Assign the following problems for students to solve. When discussing answers, call attention to comparative size of fractions multiplied and the answers. Simplify answers.

1. $\frac{2}{3}$ x $\frac{1}{2}$ 2. $\frac{2}{5}$ x $\frac{1}{3}$ 3. $\frac{2}{5}$ x $\frac{1}{3}$

4. $\frac{3}{5}$ x $\frac{2}{3}$ 5. $\frac{3}{4}$ x $\frac{2}{3}$ 6. $\frac{5}{8}$ x $\frac{1}{2}$

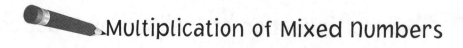

Multiplication of Mixed numbers

Students must understand that to multiply mixed numbers each mixed number must be changed to an improper fraction. Then multiply numerator times numerator and denominator times denominator. Students must change improper fraction answers back to a mixed number and simplify any fractions in the answer.

Place the following mixed number on the overhead or board.

$1\frac{1}{3}$

Tell students that to change a mixed number to an improper fraction they must first determine the denominator of the improper fraction. The denominator of the improper fraction is the-denominator in the mixed number. In the mixed number $1\frac{1}{3}$, the denominator of the fraction is 3, so the denominator of the improper fraction will be 3. Place the following diagrams on the overhead or board.

$\frac{1}{3} + \frac{1}{3} + \frac{1}{3} = 1$ $\frac{1}{3} = \frac{1}{3}$ $1 + \frac{1}{3} = \frac{4}{3} = \frac{4}{3}$

$\frac{1}{3} + \frac{1}{3} + \frac{1}{3} + \frac{1}{3}$ $= \frac{4}{3}$

Another way to determine the improper fraction is to multiply the denominator of the fraction 3 times the whole number 1 + the numerator 1. Changing the mixed number $1\frac{1}{3}$ to an improper fraction becomes

$1\frac{1}{3} = 3 \times 1 + 1 = \frac{4}{3}$

Place the mixed number $1\frac{1}{4}$ on the overhead or board. Have students change the mixed number to an improper fraction. Ask the following questions. What will the denominator of the improper fraction be? How do you know? **Place rectangle diagrams on the overhead or board so students can visualize the number of $\frac{1}{4}$ths in the mixed number $1\frac{1}{4}$.** How many $\frac{1}{4}$ths in the whole number 1? How many fourths in the fraction? Total? Also have students complete as $4 \times 1 + 1 = \frac{5}{4}$.

Have students change the following improper fractions to mixed numbers.

1. $1\frac{1}{5}$ 2. $1\frac{1}{6}$ 3. $2\frac{1}{3}$ 4. $2\frac{3}{4}$ 5. $3\frac{2}{3}$

Place the following multiplication on the overhead or board. Have students change the mixed numbers to improper fractions. Instruct students to multiply numerators and denominators. Have students convert the improper fraction answer to a mixed number with a fraction simplified.

Problem	Step 1	Step 2	Step 3	Step 4
$1\frac{1}{3} \times 1\frac{1}{4} =$	$\frac{4}{3} \times \frac{5}{4} =$	$\frac{20}{12}$ $12\overline{)20}$	$= 1\frac{8}{20}$	$= 1\frac{2}{5}$

Have students solve the following problem. Follow the above steps. Check students for understanding.

$1\frac{2}{3} \times 1\frac{1}{3}$

Assign the following problems.

1. $1\frac{1}{4} \times 1\frac{1}{2}$ 2. $1\frac{1}{3} \times 1\frac{1}{6}$ 3. $2\frac{1}{2} \times 2\frac{1}{3}$

Division of Fractions

Students must understand the term **reciprocal** before trying to divide fractions. Write the word **fraction** and **reciprocal** on the overhead or board. Write the fraction $\frac{1}{3}$ under the term fraction. Discuss what reciprocal means. Then write $\frac{3}{1}$ under the term reciprocal. Indicate that the riciprocal of $\frac{1}{3}$ is $\frac{3}{1}$. Write the following fractions under the term fraction. Have students indicate the reciprocal for each. Write the fraction and reciprocal under the proper heading as students respond.

$$\frac{1}{4} \quad \frac{1}{5} \quad \frac{1}{6} \quad \frac{2}{3} \quad \frac{3}{4} \quad \frac{1}{3} \quad \frac{4}{5} \quad \frac{5}{6}$$

Fraction	Reciprocal
$\frac{1}{3}$	$\frac{3}{1}$

Students should be taught division of fractions using the invert and multiply algorithm. Place the following problem on the overhead or board.

$$\frac{1}{3} \div \frac{1}{2}$$

Write the following on the overhead or board. **When dividing fractions the divisor is inverted and the division is rewritten as a muliplication problem. Inverting the divisor is the reciprocal. Remind students to multiply numerators and denominators after the problem is rewritten in inverted form.**

Problem	Rewritten as reciprocal	Completed problem
$\frac{1}{3} \div \frac{1}{2} =$	$\frac{1}{3} \times \frac{2}{1} =$	$\frac{1}{3} \times \frac{2}{1} = \frac{2}{3}$

Present the following problem. Have students change the improper fraction answer to a mixed number. Simplify the fraction.

$$\frac{3}{4} \div \frac{1}{6} = \qquad \frac{3}{4} \times \frac{6}{1} = \frac{18}{4} = 4\overline{)18} \qquad 4\frac{2}{4} = 4\frac{1}{2}$$

Have students solve the following problems. Follow the above steps. Change answers to mixed numbers. Simplify fractions.

1. $\frac{3}{4} \div \frac{1}{2}$ 2. $\frac{5}{6} \div \frac{1}{4}$ 3. $\frac{2}{3} \div \frac{3}{7}$

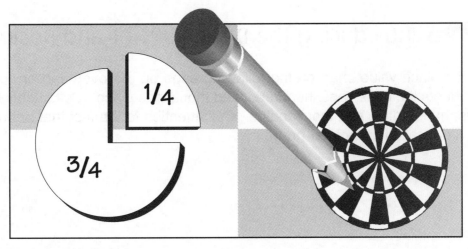

125 + 300 = 425   750 - 400 = 350   5 x (3 x 7) = 3 x (5 x 7)   3/4 - 1/4 = 1/2
5 x (3 x 7) = 3 x (5 x 7)   Understanding Decimals   125 + 300 = 425   750 - 400 = 350

Review of Place Value

When beginning the study of decimals, a review of place value is important. Place the place value diagram below on the overhead or board.

Write the number 22 on the diagram under the ones and tens. Have students tell how many ones are in 22. How many tens? What number does the 2 under the tens stand for? How many times greater is the number in the tens place than the number in the ones place? Have students write 22 in expanded notation.

20 + 2 Write in column form and add.

$$\begin{array}{r} 20 \\ + \ 2 \\ \hline 22 \end{array}$$

Thousands	Hundreds	Tens	Ones
		2	2
	2	2	2

Write the number 222 on the diagram under the ones, tens, and hundreds. Have students tell how many ones are in 222. How many tens? How many hundreds? What number does the 2 under the tens stand for? The hundreds? How many times greater is the number in the tens place than the number in the ones place? How many times greater is the 2 in the hundreds place than the 2 in the tens place. Have students write 222 in expanded notation.

200 + 20 + 2. Write in column form for students to add.

Write 2222 on the place value chart. Review the above questions including questions for the thousands place. Have students write 2222 in expanded notation 2000 + 200 + 20 + 2. Write in column form for students to add.

Have students write the following in expanded notation.

23   234   2345

Introducing the Decimal Point and Decimals

Place the place value chart on the following page on the overhead or board. Review briefly with students the ones, tens, hundreds, and thousands place. Call attention to the chart and the tenths, hundredths, and thousandths. Call attention to the fact that between the ones and tenths is a dot called a **decimal point.**

Thousands	Hundreds	Tens	Ones	.	Tenths	Hundredths	Thousandths
1	1	1	1	.			
1	1	1	1	.	1		
1	1	1	1	.	1	1	
1	1	1	1	.	1	1	1

Write the number 1111 on the chart. Have students tell the value of each numeral. Have students read the number. Then write the number 1111.1 on the chart. Read the number for the students. Have students read the number and emphasize "and" for the decimal point. Tell students the numeral in the tenths place is written .1. The decimal .1 equals the fraction $\frac{1}{10}$.

Write the number 1111.11 on the chart. Read the number for the students. Have the students read the number and emphasize "and" for the decimal point. Tell the students .11 is read as eleven hundredths. The decimal .11 equals the fraction $\frac{11}{100}$.

Have students read all three of the numbers on the chart. Emphasize the "and" when reading the decimal point.

Write the number 1111.111 on the chart. Read the number for the students. Have the students read the number and emphasize "and" for the decimal point. Tell the students .111 is read one hundred eleven thousandths. The decimal .111 equals $\frac{111}{1000}$.

Write the following on the overhead or board and have students read the numbers.

222   222.1   114.2   45.21   2345.3   67.86   267.432

Have students write the number for the following statements.
1. Seventy-eight and three tenths
2. One hundred twelve and thirty-four hundredths
3. Nine and five tenths
4. One thousand three hundred seventy-six and seven tenths
5. Fifty-four and six hundred twenty-one thousandths

Reading Numbers With Decimals

Again, put the place value chart on the board or overhead.

Place the decimals 0.1, 0.10, and 0.100 in column form on the overhead or board. Have students read the decimals.

Place the Tenths, Hundredths, and Thousandths Place Value Chart before the students. Show students that 0.1 equals one column on the tenths chart. Now show students that 0.10 equals 0.01 + 0.01 + 0.01 + 0.01 + 0.01 + 0.01 + 0.01 + 0.01 + 0.01 + 0.01 on the hundredths chart. Call attention to the fact that the area covered by 0.1 and 0.10 is exactly the same. Have students refer to the tenths and hundredths charts and use the following questions. Make sure students respond correctly to each question prior to moving to the next question.

1. One-tenth equals how many hundredths?   Write the number.
2. Two-tenths equals how many hundredths?   Write the number.
3. Three-tenths equals how many hundredths?   Write the number.
4. Four-tenths equals how many hundredths?   Write the number.
5. Five-tenths equals how many hundredths?   Write the number.
6. Six-tenths equals how many hundredths?   Write the number.
7. Seven-tenths equals how many hundredths?   Write the number.
8. Eight-tenths equals how many hundredths?   Write the number.
9. Nine-tenths equals how many hundredths?   Write the number.
10. Ten-tenths equals how many hundredths?   Write the number.

Have students write each of the above as a decimal and fraction. Use the following format.

Decimal = Fraction   Decimal = Fraction

$0.1 = \frac{1}{10}$ $0.10 = \frac{10}{100}$

$0.2 = \frac{2}{10}$ $0.20 = \frac{20}{100}$

$0.\rule{1em}{0.4pt} = \rule{2em}{0.4pt}$ $0.\rule{1em}{0.4pt} = \rule{2em}{0.4pt}$

$0.\rule{1em}{0.4pt} = \rule{2em}{0.4pt}$ $0.\rule{1em}{0.4pt} = \rule{2em}{0.4pt}$

$0.5 = \rule{2em}{0.4pt}$ $0.50 = \rule{2em}{0.4pt}$

$0.\rule{1em}{0.4pt} = \frac{6}{10}$ $0.\rule{1em}{0.4pt} = \frac{60}{100}$

$0.\rule{1em}{0.4pt} = \rule{2em}{0.4pt}$ $0.\rule{1em}{0.4pt} = \rule{2em}{0.4pt}$

$0.\rule{1em}{0.4pt} = \rule{2em}{0.4pt}$ $0.\rule{1em}{0.4pt} = \rule{2em}{0.4pt}$

$0.9 = \frac{9}{10}$ $0.90 = \frac{90}{100}$

$\rule{1em}{0.4pt}.\rule{1em}{0.4pt} = 1$ $\rule{1em}{0.4pt}.\rule{1em}{0.4pt} = 1$

Name _____   Date _____

125 + 300 = 42   750 - 400 = 350   5 x (3 x 7) = 3 x (5 x 7)   3/4 - 1/4 = 1/2
5 x (3 x 7) = 3 x (5 x 7)   Learning About Place Value 750 - 400 = 350

Learning About Place Value

1. Circle the number below that has 5 tens and 6 ones.

   65   55   56   58

2. Circle the number below that has 8 tens and 1 one.

   88   89   18   81

3. Use the following numerals and make four numbers. 1, 7, 3, 2.
   Arrange the numbers on the blanks below from largest to smallest.

   a. _____   b. _____   c. _____   d. _____

4. The largest place value that can be made with the four numbers in #3 is
   a. hundreds   b. tens   c. thousands   d. ones

5. The smallest number made will have the numeral __ in the thousands place.
   a. 7   b. 3   c. 1   d. 2

6. The largest number made will have the numeral __ in the thousands place.
   a. 7   b. 3   c. 1   d. 2

7. Place each of the numbers you made in #3 under the correct headings below.

Thousands	Hundreds	Tens	Ones
a. _____	a. _____	a. _____	a. _____
b. _____	b. _____	b. _____	b. _____
c. _____	c. _____	c. _____	c. _____
d. _____	d. _____	d. _____	d. _____

Name _____   Date _____

Understanding More About Place Value

Complete the following.

1. 14 = _____ tens _____ ones
2. 10 = _____ tens _____ ones
3. 73 = _____ tens _____ ones
4. 89 = _____ tens _____ ones
5. 123 = _____ hundreds _____ tens _____ ones
6. 345 = _____ hundreds _____ tens _____ ones
7. 908 = _____ hundreds _____ tens _____ ones
8. 1356 = _____ thousands _____ hundreds _____ tens _____ ones
9. 7654 = _____ thousands _____ hundreds _____ tens _____ ones
10. 9045 = _____ thousands _____ hundreds _____ tens _____ ones

Improving In Understanding of Place Value

On the blanks below write the largest and smallest number possible using the numbers. 1, 7, and 6.

_____ largest number   _____ smallest number

1. The numeral in the hundreds place is: _____ largest number_____ smallest number.

2. The value of the numeral in the hundreds place is: _____ largest number; _____ smallest number.

3. The numeral in the tens place is: _____ largest number; _____ smallest number.

4. The value of the numeral in the tens place is: _____ largest number; _____ smallest number.

5. The numeral in the ones place is: _____ largest number; _____ smallest number.

6. The value of the numeral in the ones place is: _____ largest number; _____ smallest number.

Name _____   Date _____

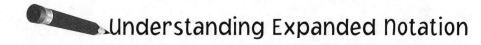# Understanding Expanded Notation

Rewrite each of the following numbers using expanded notation form. The first one has been completed for you.

Number	Expanded Notation Form
347	(3 x 100) + (4 x 10) + (7 x 1)

1. 486   _____

2. 786   _____

3. 1923   _____

4. 2543   _____

5. 124   _____

6. 241   _____

7. 421   _____

8. 12   _____

9. 21   _____

10. 401   _____

11. 140   _____

12. 54   _____

13. 743   _____

14. 2675   _____

Name _____   Date _____

125 + 300 = 42~~   750 - 400 = 350   5 x (3 x 7) = 3 x (5 x 7)   3/4 - 1/4 = 1/2
5 x (3 x 7) = 3 x (5 x 7)   Learning About Exponents   750 - 400 = 350

Understanding Exponents in Base Ten

Complete the following table. Rewrite each of the numbers as a base number with an exponent. The first one has been completed.

Number	Base Number	Exponent	Base Number/ Exponent
1. 2	2	1	2^1
2. 4			
3. 8			
4. 16			
5. 32			
6. 64			

Complete the following table. On the blank write the number that each base and exponent represents.

Base/Exponent	Number
7. 10^0	
8. 10^1	
9. 10^2	
10. 10^3	
11. 10^4	
12. 10^5	
13. 10^6	
14. 10^7	
15. 10^8	

Name _____ Date _____

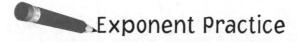 **Exponent Practice**

Complete the blanks in the table below. Rewrite each of the number statements as the number it equals. Then write the number as a base with an exponent. The first one has been completed for you.

Number Statement	Number	Base Number With Exponent
1. 3 x 3 x 3	27	3^3
2. 4 x 4	_____	_____
3. 10 x 10 x 10 x 10 x 10	_____	_____
4. 2 x 2 x 2 x 2 x 2 x 2 x 2	_____	_____
5. 6 x 6 x 6 x 6	_____	_____
6. 8 x 8 x 8	_____	_____
7. 11 x 11	_____	_____
8. 12 x 12 x 12 x 12 x 12	_____	_____
9. 4 x 4 x 4 x 4 x 4 x 4	_____	_____
10. 5 x 5 x 5 x 5 x 5	_____	_____

Complete the blanks in the following selection.

11. The base number and exponent 2^3 can be written as the number _____.

12. The number 36 can be written with a base number and exponent as _____.

13. The base number _____ with the exponent ^{3} equals the number 125.

14. The base number _____ with the exponent ^{6} equals the number 64.

15. The base number _____ with the exponent ^{4} equals the number 625.

16. The base number 5 with the exponent zero equals the number _____.

17. The base number and exponent 4^1 equals the number _____.

18. The base number and exponent is 10^5. The base number is _____. The exponent is _____.

19. Write 10 x 10 as a base number with an exponent. _____.

20. Write 2 x 2 x 2 x 2 as a base number with an exponent. _____.

21. Write 3 x 3 x 3 x 3 x 3 x 3 x 3 as a base number with an exponent. _____.

22. To change 6^3 to 216 it is necessary to multiply/divide/add/subtract. (circle one)

Name _____   Date _____

Learning About Base Five and Base Ten

Write the value of each of the base ten numbers as a base five number. Some have been completed for you.

1. Base Ten: 1   2   3   4   5   6   7   8   9   10   11   12   13
   Base Five: __   __   __   __   10   __   __   13   __   20   __   __   __

   Base Ten: 14   15   16   17   18   19   20   21   22   23   24   25
   Base Five: __   30   __   __   __   __   __   __   __   __   __   __

Change each of the following Base Five numbers to a Base Ten number. The first one has been completed for you.

2. $123_5 = (1 \times 25) + (2 \times 5) + (3 \times 1) = 38_{10}$

3. $124_5 = ($ x $) + ($ x $) + ($ x $) =$ _____$_{10}$

4. $122_5 =$

5. $211_5 =$

6. $301_5 =$

7. $312_5 =$

8. $422_5 =$

9. $111_5 =$

10. $2222_5 =$

Name _____ Date _____

$$125 + 300 = 425 \quad 75 \ \bullet \ 400 = 350 \quad 5 \times (3 \times 7) = 3 \times (5 \times 7) \quad 3/4 - 1/4 = 1/2$$
$$5 \times (3 \times 7) = 3 \times (5 \times 7) \quad \text{Review Lessons} \quad = 425 \quad 750 - 400 = 350$$

Place Value, Expanded notation, Exponents, Base Ten, Base Five

1. Write the number that has six hundreds, five tens, and three ones. _____

2. Write the number that has four thousands, three hundreds, zero tens, and four ones. _____.

3. If you write the largest number possible with the numerals 4, 8, 3, 2, the numeral _____ will be in the thousands place.

4. If you write the largest number possible with the numerals 4, 9, 2, 6, the numeral _____ will be in the tens place.

5. The following numbers are written in expanded notation. Write the number on the blank that each expanded notation equals.

    a. (3 x 100) + (2 x 10) + (6 x 1) = _____

    b. (5 x 1000) + (9 x 100) + (3 x 10) + (6 x 1) = _____

    c. (2 x 1000) + (0 x 100) + (4 x 10) + (2 x 1) = _____

    d. (9 x 1000) + (0 x 100) + (0 x 10) + (0 x 1) = _____

6. Rewrite each of the following with a base and exponent.

    a.   10 x 10 x 10 = _____

    b.   2 x 2 x 2 x 2 = _____

    c.   5 x 5 = _____

    d.   3 x 3 x 3 x 3 x 3 = _____

    e.   4 x 4 x 4 = _____

7. Write the number on the blank that the base number and exponent equal. (Base Ten)

    a. 2^4 = _____

    b. 7^2 = _____

    c. 4^3 = _____

    d. 10^3 = _____

    e. 5^4 = _____

8. Each of the following numbers is a Base Five number. Change each Base Five number to a Base Ten value. The first one has been completed for you.

   a. $111_5 = (1 \times 25) + (1 \times 5) + (1 \times 1) = 31_{10}$

   b. $110_5 = ($ ___ $\times$ ___ $) + ($ ___ $\times$ ___ $) + ($ ___ $\times$ ___ $) = $ _____ $_{10}$

   c. $101_5 = $ _____ $ + $ _____ $ + $ _____ $ = $ _____ $_{10}$

   d. $232_5 = $ _____ ___ _____ ___ _____ $ = $ _____

   e. $311_5 = $ _____ ___ _____ ___ _____ $ = $ _____

   f. $201_5 = $ _____ ___ _____ ___ _____ $ = $ _____

   g. $222_5 = $ _____ ___ _____ ___ _____ $ = $ _____

   h. $144_5 = $ _____ ___ _____ ___ _____ $ = $ _____

   i. $1423_5 = $ _____ ___ _____ ___ _____ $ = $ _____

9. Each of the following numbers is in Base Five. Rewrite the Base Five number as a Base Ten number.

Base Five	equals	Base Ten
a. 11_5		_____
b. 12_5		_____
c. 245_5		_____
d. 33_5		_____
e. 123_5		_____

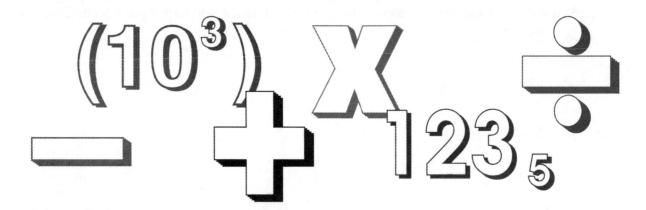

Name _____   Date _____

125 + 300 = 425   750 - 400 = 350   5 x (3 x 7) = 3 x (5 x 7)   3/4 - 1/4 = 1/2
5 x (3 x 7) = 3 x (5 x 7)   Learning About Addition   750 - 400 = 350

 Checking Understanding of Addition

Complete the following addition problems. Rewrite each addition problem using expanded notation. The first one has been completed.

1.   54 = 5 tens and 4 ones = 50 + 4
    +32 = 3 tens and 2 ones = 30 + 2
     86 = 8 tens and 6 ones = 80 + 6

2.   62 = ___ tens and ___ ones = ___ + ___
    +27 = ___ tens and ___ ones = ___ + ___
    ___ = ___ tens and ___ ones = ___ + ___

3.   85 = ___ tens and ___ ones = ___ + ___
    +14 = ___ tens and ___ ones = ___ + ___
    ___ = ___ tens and ___ ones = ___ + ___

4.   9 = ___ tens and ___ ones = ___ + ___
     +9 = ___ tens and ___ ones = ___ + ___
    ___ = ___ tens and ___ ones = ___ + ___

5.   88 = ___ tens and ___ ones = ___ + ___
    +11 = ___ tens and ___ ones = ___ + ___
    ___ = ___ tens and ___ ones = ___ + ___

6.   124 = ___ hundreds ___ tens and ___ ones = ___ + ___ + ___
    +164 = ___ hundreds ___ tens and ___ ones = ___ + ___ + ___
     ___ = ___ hundreds ___ tens and ___ ones = ___ + ___ + ___

7.   456 = ___ hundreds ___ tens and ___ ones = ___ + ___ + ___
    +342 = ___ hundreds ___ tens and ___ ones = ___ + ___ + ___
     ___ = ___ hundreds ___ tens and ___ ones = ___ + ___ + ___

Name _____   Date _____

Checking Skills in Regrouping

Learning how to regroup is an important skill in becoming a better math student. Review the following regrouping example before completing the problems below.

Step 1   Step 2   Step 3
                                                                    1
Example: 68 = 6 tens and 8 ones   68   68   take the 1 ten
         +14 = 1 ten   and 4 ones   +14   +14   to the ones
          82 = 7 tens and 12 ones; 12 ones = 1 ten and 2 ones   82   column and add

Add the following problems. It will be necessary that you regroup when adding these problems.

1. Step 1   Step 2   Step 3
      78 =   ___ tens and ___ ones   or   ___
     +13 =   + ___ tens and ___ ones   or   + ___
                            ___ tens and ___ ones   or   ___

2. Step 1   Step 2   Step 3
      67 =   ___ hundreds, ___ tens and ___ ones   or   ___
     +47 =   + ___ hundreds, ___ tens and ___ ones   or   + ___
                            ___ hundreds, ___ tens and ___ ones   or   ___

3. 346   4. 594   5. 678   6. 148   7. 422
   + 236   + 219   + 342   + 873   + 578

8. 23 + 21 + 13 = _____   9. 23 + 26 + 13 = _____   10. 33 + 46 + 13 = _____

11. 245   12. 245   13. 245   14. 245   15. 245   16. 245
     231   232   233   234   235   236
     211   212   213   214   215   216
   + 311   + 311   + 311   + 311   + 311   + 311

17. Does 23 + 45 = 45 + 23   yes/no
18. Does 345 + 567 = 567 + 345   yes/no
19. Does 89 + 413 + 267 + 12 = 12 + 267 + 413 + 89   yes/no

Name _____   Date _____

More Addition Practice

1. 23
   + 11

2. 46
   + 33

3. 36
   + 15

4. 54
   + 34

5. 24
   + 15

6. 57
   + 38

7. 86
   + 77

8. 78
   + 69

9. 278
   + 142

10. 323
    + 213

11. 487
    + 466

12. 195
    + 184

13. 323
    + 428

14. 416
    + 607

15. 907
    + 178

16. 784
    + 275

17. 48
    79
   + 14

18. 33
    12
    97
   + 62

19. 281
    407
   + 899

20. 727
    351
    490
   + 118

Name _____   Date _____

125 + 300 = ___   750 - 400 = 350   5 x (3 x 7) = 3 x (5 x 7)   3/4 - 1/4 = 1/2
5 x (3 x 7) = 3 x (5 x 7)   ___ Learning About Subtraction   750 - 400 = 350

Checking Skills in Subtraction

Complete the following subtraction problems. Rewrite each subtraction problem using expanded notation. The first one has been completed.

1.   54 = 5 tens and 4 ones = 50 + 4
    - 32 = 3 tens and 2 ones = 30 + 2
    22 = 2 tens and 2 ones = 20 + 2

2.   62 = ___ tens and ___ ones = ___ + ___
    - 21 = ___ tens and ___ ones = ___ + ___
    ___ = ___ tens and ___ ones = ___ + ___

3.   85 = ___ tens and ___ ones = ___ + ___
    - 14 = ___ tens and ___ ones = ___ + ___
    ___ = ___ tens and ___ ones = ___ + ___

4.   9 = ___ tens and ___ ones = ___ + ___
    - 9 = ___ tens and ___ ones = ___ + ___
    ___ = ___ tens and ___ ones = ___ + ___

5.   88 = ___ tens and ___ ones = ___ + ___
    - 11 = ___ tens and ___ ones = ___ + ___
    ___ = ___ tens and ___ ones = ___ + ___

6.   164 = ___ hundreds, ___ tens and ___ ones = ___ + ___
    - 124 = ___ hundreds, ___ tens and ___ ones = ___ + ___
    ___ = ___ hundreds, ___ tens and ___ ones = ___ + ___

7.   456 = ___ hundreds, ___ tens and ___ ones = ___ + ___
    - 342 = ___ hundreds, ___ tens and ___ ones = ___ + ___
    ___ = ___ hundreds, ___ tens and ___ ones = ___ + ___

Name _____ Date _____

 Checking Skills in Regrouping

When subtracting, it is often necessary to regroup.

Example 1: Regrouping tens to ones.

Step 1 Problem	Step 2 Expanded Notation	Step 3 Regroup
Subtract $4\overset{6}{7}\overset{17}{7}$	or 400 + 70 + 7	= 400 + 60 + 17
-219	200 + 10 + 9	= -200 + 10 + 9
258		200 + 50 + 8 = 258

So 477 - 219 = 258

Checking the Answer: 258 + 219 = 477

Example 2: Regrouping hundreds to tens to ones.

Step 1 Problem	Step 2 Expanded Notation	Step 3 Regroup
Subtract $\overset{2}{3}\overset{13}{4}\overset{17}{7}$	or 300 + 40 + 7	= 200 +130 + 17
-258	or 200 + 50 + 8	= -200 + 50 + 8
89		80 + 9 = 89

So 347 - 258 = 89

Checking the Answer: 258 + 89 = 347

Subtract the following problems. It will be necessary that you regroup when subtracting these problems.

1.

Step 1 Problem	Step 2 Expanded Notation	Step 3 Regroup
78	or +	=
-19	+	=_____
		= ____

So 78 - 19 = _____

Checking the Answer: _____ + _____ = 78

2.

Step 1 Problem	Step 2 Expanded Notation	Step 3 Regroup
67	or +	=
-48	+	=_____
		= ____

So 67 - 48 = _____

Checking the Answer: _____ + _____ = 67

Name _____   Date _____

3.   Step 1   Step 2   Step 3
      Problem   Expanded Notation   Regroup

           86   or   +   = _____
          -67   +   = _____
                                                                    = ____

So 86 - 67 = _____

Checking the Answer: _____ + _____ = _____

4.   346
     -236   Checking the Answer: _____ + _____ = 346

5.   594
     -219   Checking the Answer: _____ + _____ = _____

6.   678
     -342   Checking the Answer: _____ + _____ = _____

7.   876
     -786   Checking the Answer: _____ + _____ = _____

8.   978
     -789   Checking the Answer: _____ + _____ = _____

9. 87 - 44 = _____   10. 145 - 78 = _____   11. 788 - 699 = _____

Name _____ Date _____

 More Subtraction Practice

1. 23 - 11	2. 46 - 33	3. 36 - 15	4. 54 - 34
5. 24 - 15	6. 57 - 38	7. 86 - 77	8. 78 - 69
9. 278 - 142	10. 323 - 213	11. 487 - 466	12. 195 - 184
13. 323 - 245	14. 416 - 238	15. 907 - 789	16. 784 - 691

 Addition and Subtraction Practice

Solve the following problems. Watch for the **signs** that tell you what to do.

1. The + sign tells me to find the __ __ __.

2. When I find the __ __ __, I must add.

3. The - sign tells me to find the __ __ __ __ __ __ __ __ __ __.

4. When I find the __ __ __ __ __ __ __ __ __ __ __, I must subtract.

5. 35 + 36	6. 789 - 654	7. 875 + 117	8. 3456 - 2365
9. 588 - 499	10. 623 + 798	11. 4673 - 3785	12. 6021 + 4598

Name _____   Date _____

$125 + 300 = 4$ $750 - 400 = 350$ $5 \times (3 \times 7) = 3 \times (5 \times 7)$ $3/4 - 1/4 = 1/2$

Learning About Multiplication

$5 \times (3 \times 7) = 3 \times (5 \times 7)$ $125 + 300 = 425$ $750 - 400 = 350$

Multiplication: The Associative Property

1. $(3 \times 5) \times 6 = 3 \times (5 \times 6) = $ _____ $\times 6 = 3 \times$ _____

2. $5 \times (4 \times 5) = (5 \times 4) \times 5 = 5 \times$ _____ $=$ _____ $\times 5$

3. $(8 \times 4) \times 10 = 8 \times (4 \times 10) = $ _____ $\times 10 = 8 \times$ _____

4. $9 \times (3 \times 7) = (9 \times 3) \times 7 = 9 \times$ _____ $=$ _____ $\times 7$

5. $20 \times (6 \times 4) = (20 \times 6) 4 = 20 \times$ _____ $=$ _____ $\times 4$

6. $(14 \times 25) \times 4 = 14 \times (25 \times 4) = $ _____ $\times$ _____ $=$ _____ $\times$ _____

7. $(35 \times 15) \times 30 = 35 \times (15 \times 30) = $ _____ $\times$ _____ $=$ _____ $\times$ _____

8. $8 \times (50 \times 4) = (8 \times 50) \times 4 = $ _____ $\times$ _____ $=$ _____ $\times$ _____

9. $(7 \times 24) \times 5 = 7 \times (24 \times 5) = $ _____ $\times$ _____ $=$ _____ $\times$ _____

10. $52 \times (12 \times 5) = (52 \times 12) \times 5 = $ _____ $\times$ _____ $=$ _____ $\times$ _____

11. $8 \times 5 \times 6 \times 3 = $ _____

12. $(8 \times 5) \times (6 \times 3) = $ _____ $\times$ _____ $=$ _____

13. $12 \times 4 \times 18 \times 5 = $ _____

14. $(12 \times 4) \times (18 \times 5) = $ _____ $\times$ _____ $=$ _____

15. $45 \times 5 \times 10 \times 5 = $ _____

16. $(45 \times 5) \times (10 \times 5) = $ _____ $\times$ _____ $=$ _____

17. $23 \times 7 \times 45 \times 6 = $ _____

18. $(23 \times 7) \times (45 \times 6) = $ _____ $\times$ _____ $=$ _____

19. $31 \times 9 \times 12 \times 8 = $ _____

20. $(31 \times 9) \times (12 \times 8) = $ _____ $\times$ _____ $=$ _____

Name _____   Date _____

Multiplication: The Distributive Property

Complete the following problems.

1. 4 x 11 = 4(5 + 6) = 4 x 5 + 4 x 6 = _____ + _____ = _____

2. 8 x 24 = 8(20 + 4) = 8 x 20 + 8 x 4 = _____ + _____ = _____

3. 7 x 36 = __(30 + 6) = __ x 30 + __ x 6 = _____ + _____ = _____

4. 3 x 11 = __(__ + 8) = __ x __ + __ x __ = _____ + _____ = _____

5. 3 x 17 = 3(7 + 10) = 3 x __ + 3 x __ = _____ + _____ = _____

6. 5 x 38 = __(30 + 8) = 5 x __ + 5 x __ = _____ + _____ = _____

7. 8 x 75 = 8(__ + 5) = __ x __ + __ x __ = _____ + _____ = _____

8. 12 x 120 = __(100 + 20) = __ x __ + __ x __ = _____ + _____ = _____

9. 25 x 150 = __(__ + 50) = __ x __ + __ x __ = _____ + _____ = _____

10. 85 x 69 = __(60 + __) = __ x __ + __ x __ = _____ + _____ = _____

Multiplication Practice

1. 23 x 3	2. 321 x 4	3. 231 x 2	4. 1111 x 9	5. 31 x 2	6. 434 x 2
7. 3111 x 3	8. 9876 x 1	9. 32 x 4	10. 623 x 3	11. 5323 x 3	12. 722 x 4

Developing Regrouping Skills

1. 43 x 5	2. 743 x 6	3. 6431 x 8	4. 8743 x 9	5. 67 x 8	6. 854 x 7
7. 906 x 7	8. 5764 x 6	9. 80 x 5	10. 607 x 8	11. 4007 x 3	12. 5040 x 9

Name _____ Date _____

Regrouping Using Larger Numbers

1. 34
    x 21

2. 64
    x 11

3. 134
    x 12

4. 524
    x 10

5. 53
    x 22

6. 411
    x 33

7. 4102
    x 13

8. 3333
    x 11

9. 34
    x 32

10. 65
     x 53

11. 78
     x 40

12. 87
     x 64

13. 68
     x 61

14. 89
     x 24

15. 74
     x 54

16. 99
     x 34

17. 231
     x 45

18. 456
     x 74

19. 345
     x 63

20. 781
     x 54

21. 642
     x 78

22. 193
     x 88

23. 572
     x 340

24. 916
     x 721

Name _____   Date _____

Learning About Division

Checking Understanding of Division

1. $3\overline{)9}$ 2. $4\overline{)8}$ 3. $7\overline{)14}$ 4. $6\overline{)18}$

5. $4\overline{)24}$ 6. $6\overline{)30}$ 7. $5\overline{)15}$ 8. $5\overline{)25}$

9. $3\overline{)27}$ 10. $6\overline{)24}$ 11. $7\overline{)42}$ 12. $9\overline{)54}$

13. $4\overline{)32}$ 14. $11\overline{)88}$ 15. $7\overline{)63}$ 16. $8\overline{)72}$

17. $63 \div 7 =$ _____   18. $48 \div 8 =$ _____

19. $81 \div 9 =$ _____   20. $66 \div 3 =$ _____

Name _____   Date _____

Understanding Division With Remainders

1. $9\overline{)64}$ 2. $5\overline{)27}$ 3. $6\overline{)32}$ 4. $5\overline{)24}$

5. $9\overline{)37}$ 6. $4\overline{)38}$ 7. $7\overline{)45}$ 8. $3\overline{)71}$

9. $14 \div 3 =$ _____   10. $79 \div 5 =$ _____   11. $51 \div 6 =$ _____   12. $107 \div 9 =$ _____

One- and Two-Digit Divisors Without Remainders

1. $3\overline{)69}$ 2. $4\overline{)84}$ 3. $5\overline{)90}$ 4. $7\overline{)77}$

5. $7\overline{)126}$ 6. $4\overline{)148}$ 7. $5\overline{)215}$ 8. $8\overline{)648}$

9. $25\overline{)125}$ 10. $26\overline{)78}$ 11. $18\overline{)198}$ 12. $31\overline{)372}$

13. $324 \div 36 =$ ____   14. $420 \div 15 =$ ____   15. $529 \div 23 =$ ____   16. $352 \div 16 =$ ____

Name _____   Date _____

Two-Digit Divisors With Remainders

1. 14)270   2. 41)286   3. 24)627   4. 68)395

5. 29)413   6. 13)865   7. 14)951   8. 58)297

9. 23)789   10. 17)643   11. 45)952   12. 56)498

13. 65)391   14. 34)267   15. 25)536   16. 21)800

17. 841 ÷ 22 = ____   18. 611 ÷ 43 = ____   19. 123 ÷ 87 = ____   20. 387 ÷ 17 = ____

21. 369 ÷ 16 = ____   22. 433 ÷ 15 = ____   23. 322 ÷ 36 = ____   24. 526 ÷ 23 = ____

Name _____   Date _____

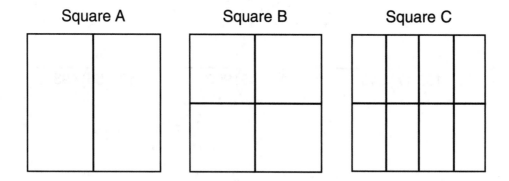

125 + 300 = 4?5   750 - 400 = 350   5 x (3 x 7) = 3 x (5 x 7)   3/4 - 1/4 = 1/2
5 x (3 x 7) = 3 x (5 x 7)   ?/4 - 1/4 = 1/2   125 + 300 = 425   750 - 400 = 350
Learning About Fractions

Learning About Simple Fractions

Each of the following squares has been divided into equal parts. Answer the following questions.

1. What fraction does each part represent in square A? _____

2. What fraction does each part represent in square B? _____

3. What fraction does each part represent in square C? _____

Square A   Square B   Square C

4. Divide Square D into equal parts so that each part equals the fraction $\frac{1}{16}$.

Square D

5. Label each part in Square D with the fraction the part represents as a part of Square D.

Name _____ Date _____

6. Divide Square E into 32 equal fraction parts. Each fraction part will equal the fraction _____.

Square E

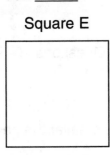

7. Divide Circle F into 32 equal fraction parts. Each fraction part will equal the fraction _____.

Circle F

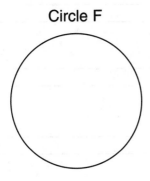

8. If **each** of the fraction parts in Circle F were divided into four equal fraction parts, Circle F would then have A) ___ fraction parts. Each fraction part would equal the fraction B) _____.

9. Divide Diagram G into 32 equal fraction parts. Each fraction part will equal the fraction _____.

Diagram G

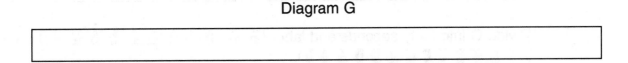

Refer to Squares A, B, C, D, and E on page 74 and 75 and answer the following questions.

10. Each fraction part in Square A equals the fraction _____.

11. Each fraction part in Square B equals the fraction _____.

12. Each fraction part in Square C equals the fraction _____.

Name _____ Date _____

13. Each fraction part in Square D equals the fraction _____.

14. Each fraction part in Square E equals the fraction _____.

15. Complete the following blanks and arrange the fractions in Questions 10–14 in order from largest to smallest.

_____   _____   _____   _____   _____

16. T/F   In the above fractions, the larger the denominator the smaller the part the fraction equals.

17. Divide the following diagram into fraction parts.
    Divide A into halves and label ($\frac{1}{2}$ $\frac{2}{2}$).

A [   ]

Divide B into fourths and label ($\frac{1}{4}$ $\frac{2}{4}$ $\frac{3}{4}$ $\frac{4}{4}$).

B [   ]

Divide C into sixths and label ($\frac{1}{6}$ $\frac{2}{6}$ $\frac{3}{6}$ $\frac{4}{6}$ $\frac{5}{6}$ $\frac{6}{6}$).

C [   ]

Divide D into eighths and label ($\frac{1}{8}$ $\frac{2}{8}$ $\frac{3}{8}$ $\frac{4}{8}$ $\frac{5}{8}$ $\frac{6}{8}$ $\frac{7}{8}$ $\frac{8}{8}$).

D [   ]

Divide E into twelfths and label ($\frac{1}{12}$ $\frac{2}{12}$ $\frac{3}{12}$ $\frac{4}{12}$ $\frac{5}{12}$ $\frac{6}{12}$ $\frac{7}{12}$ $\frac{8}{12}$ $\frac{9}{12}$ $\frac{10}{12}$ $\frac{11}{12}$ $\frac{12}{12}$).

E [   ]

Divide F into sixteenths and label ($\frac{1}{16}$ $\frac{2}{16}$ $\frac{3}{16}$ $\frac{4}{16}$ $\frac{5}{16}$ $\frac{6}{16}$ $\frac{7}{16}$ $\frac{8}{16}$ $\frac{9}{16}$ $\frac{10}{16}$ $\frac{11}{16}$ $\frac{12}{16}$ $\frac{13}{16}$ $\frac{14}{16}$ $\frac{15}{16}$ $\frac{16}{16}$).

F [   ]

Divide G into thirty-seconds and label ($\frac{1}{32}$ $\frac{2}{32}$ $\frac{3}{32}$ $\frac{4}{32}$ $\frac{5}{32}$ $\frac{6}{32}$ $\frac{7}{32}$ $\frac{8}{32}$ $\frac{9}{32}$ $\frac{10}{32}$ $\frac{11}{32}$ $\frac{12}{32}$ $\frac{13}{32}$ $\frac{14}{32}$ $\frac{15}{32}$ $\frac{16}{32}$ $\frac{17}{32}$ $\frac{18}{32}$ $\frac{19}{32}$ $\frac{20}{32}$ $\frac{21}{32}$ $\frac{22}{32}$ $\frac{23}{32}$ $\frac{24}{32}$ $\frac{25}{32}$ $\frac{26}{32}$ $\frac{27}{32}$ $\frac{28}{32}$ $\frac{29}{32}$ $\frac{30}{32}$ $\frac{31}{32}$ $\frac{32}{32}$).

G [   ]

Name _____   Date _____

Refer to the diagrams on page 76 and answer the following questions.

18. $\frac{1}{2} = \frac{}{4}$ 19. $\frac{1}{2} = \frac{}{8}$ 20. $\frac{1}{2} = \frac{}{16}$ 21. $\frac{1}{2} = \frac{}{32}$

22. $\frac{1}{4} = \frac{}{8}$ 23. $\frac{1}{4} = \frac{}{16}$ 24. $\frac{1}{4} = \frac{}{32}$ 25. $\frac{1}{8} = \frac{}{16}$

26. $\frac{3}{4} = \frac{}{8}$ 27. $\frac{3}{4} = \frac{}{16}$ 28. $\frac{3}{4} = \frac{}{32}$ 29. $\frac{3}{8} = \frac{}{16}$

30. $\frac{5}{8} = \frac{}{16}$ 31. $\frac{5}{6} = \frac{}{12}$

Match the following fractions with the fraction listed in the following questions.

$\frac{2}{8}$ $\frac{4}{8}$ $\frac{6}{8}$ $\frac{4}{16}$ $\frac{8}{16}$ $\frac{9}{12}$ $\frac{8}{32}$ $\frac{16}{32}$ $\frac{24}{32}$

32. $\frac{1}{4} =$ _____   _____   _____

33. $\frac{1}{2} =$ _____   _____   _____

34. $\frac{3}{4} =$ _____   _____   _____

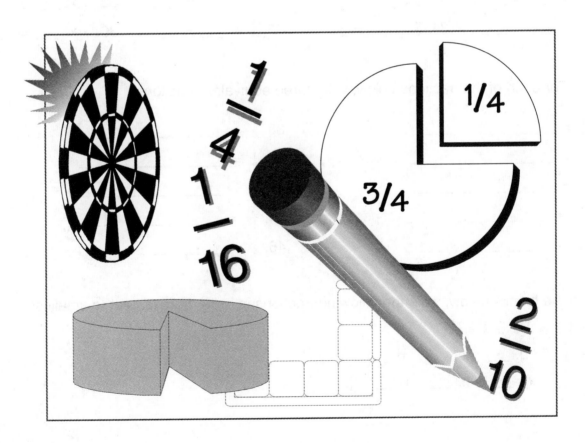

Name _____ Date _____

Learning About Equivalent Fractions

Change each of the following to an equivalent fraction.

1. $\frac{1}{8}$ x $\frac{3}{3}$ _____   2. $\frac{1}{8}$ x $\frac{2}{2}$ _____   3. $\frac{1}{8}$ x $\frac{4}{4}$ _____   4. $\frac{1}{2}$ x $\frac{4}{4}$ _____

5. $\frac{1}{2}$ x $\frac{3}{3}$ _____   6. $\frac{1}{2}$ x $\frac{2}{2}$ _____   7. $\frac{1}{4}$ x $\frac{2}{2}$ _____   8. $\frac{1}{4}$ x $\frac{3}{3}$ _____

9. $\frac{1}{4}$ x $\frac{5}{5}$ _____   10. $\frac{1}{3}$ x $\frac{3}{3}$ _____   11. $\frac{1}{3}$ x $\frac{4}{4}$ _____   12. $\frac{1}{3}$ x $\frac{2}{2}$ _____

Change each of the following to an equivalent fraction.

13. $\frac{3}{4}$ x $\frac{2}{2}$ _____   14. $\frac{2}{3}$ x $\frac{4}{4}$ _____   15. $\frac{3}{8}$ x $\frac{3}{3}$ _____   16. $\frac{5}{8}$ x $\frac{2}{2}$ _____

17. $\frac{3}{10}$ x $\frac{3}{3}$ _____   18. $\frac{4}{8}$ x $\frac{2}{2}$ _____   19. $\frac{1}{16}$ x $\frac{2}{2}$ _____   20. $\frac{7}{8}$ x $\frac{4}{4}$ _____

21. $\frac{3}{5}$ x $\frac{2}{2}$ _____   22. $\frac{5}{6}$ x $\frac{4}{4}$ _____   23. $\frac{2}{5}$ x $\frac{2}{2}$ _____   24. $\frac{3}{4}$ x $\frac{3}{3}$ _____

Change each of the folloiwng to an equivalent fraction.

25. $\frac{2}{3}$ x ___ = ___   26. $\frac{1}{2}$ x ___ = ___   27. $\frac{1}{3}$ x ___ = ___   28. $\frac{3}{4}$ x ___ = ___

29. $\frac{7}{10}$ x ___ = ___   30. $\frac{5}{8}$ x ___ = ___   31. $\frac{5}{6}$ x ___ = ___   32. $\frac{3}{5}$ x ___ = ___

33. $\frac{3}{16}$ x ___ = ___   34. $\frac{3}{8}$ x ___ = ___   35. $\frac{3}{9}$ x ___ = ___   36. $\frac{1}{6}$ x ___ = ___

For each of the fractions below, write three equivalent fractions.

37. $\frac{1}{2}$ = _____ _____ _____   38. $\frac{1}{3}$ = _____ _____ _____

39. $\frac{1}{4}$ = _____ _____ _____   40. $\frac{1}{6}$ = _____ _____ _____

41. $\frac{1}{8}$ = _____ _____ _____   42. $\frac{1}{9}$ = _____ _____ _____

43. $\frac{1}{10}$ = _____ _____ _____   44. $\frac{1}{12}$ = _____ _____ _____

45. $\frac{1}{16}$ = _____ _____ _____   46. $\frac{1}{5}$ = _____ _____ _____

47. On the blanks below, write the following fractions in order from largest to smallest.

$\frac{1}{10}$ $\frac{1}{2}$ $\frac{1}{3}$ $\frac{1}{12}$ $\frac{1}{4}$ $\frac{1}{6}$ $\frac{1}{16}$ $\frac{1}{8}$ $\frac{1}{9}$ $\frac{1}{5}$

a. ___   b. ___   c. ___   d. ___   e. ___

f. ___   g. ___   h. ___   i. ___   j. ___

Name _____   Date _____

Reviewing Fractions

Place each of the following fractions correctly on the line. Answer the questions that follow.

1. Place $\frac{3}{8}$ and $\frac{1}{2}$ on the line.

├─────────────────────────────────┤

2. $\frac{3}{8}$ is (greater/less) than $\frac{1}{2}$.

3. Place $\frac{5}{8}$ and $\frac{1}{2}$ on the line.

├─────────────────────────────────┤

4. $\frac{5}{8}$ is (greater/less) than $\frac{1}{2}$.

5. Place $\frac{7}{16}$ and $\frac{1}{4}$ on the line.

├─────────────────────────────────┤

6. $\frac{7}{16}$ is (greater/less) than $\frac{1}{4}$.

7. Place $\frac{3}{4}$ and $\frac{1}{4}$ on the line.

├─────────────────────────────────┤

8. $\frac{3}{4}$ is (greater/less) than $\frac{1}{4}$.

9. Place $\frac{3}{4}$ and $\frac{8}{16}$ on the line.

├─────────────────────────────────┤

10. $\frac{3}{4}$ is (greater/less) than $\frac{8}{16}$.

11. Place $\frac{2}{3}$ and $\frac{7}{9}$ on the line.

├─────────────────────────────────┤

12. $\frac{2}{3}$ is (greater/less) than $\frac{7}{9}$.

Answer the following. Use the fraction lines below if needed.

├──┤

├──┤

13. Five-eighths is (greater/less) than one-half.
14. Three-fourths is (greater/less) than three-eighths.
15. Two-thirds is (greater/less) than one-half.
16. Three-sixteenths is (greater/less) than three-eighths.
17. One-fifth is (greater/less) than one-half.
18. Three-fourths is (greater/less) than five-sixths.
19. Two-thirds is (greater/less) than five-sixths.
20. One-sixteenth is (greater/less) than five-sixths.
21. Three-fifths is (greater/less) than one-half.
22. Three-fourths is (greater/less) than three-fifths.
23. Three-sixths is (greater/less) than five-eighths.
24. Three-tenths is (greater/less) than one-fifth.

Name _____ Date _____

 Learning About Improper Fractions

Complete the following blanks. The first one has been completed for you.

1. $\frac{8}{3} = \frac{3}{3} + \frac{3}{3} + \frac{2}{3} = 2\frac{2}{3}$
   $\frac{8}{3} = 1 + 1 + \frac{2}{3} = 2\frac{2}{3}$

   $\frac{8}{3} = 8 \div 3 = 3\overline{)8}^{\,2} = 2\frac{2}{3}$
   $\phantom{\frac{8}{3} = 8 \div 3 = 3)}\underline{6}$
   $\phantom{\frac{8}{3} = 8 \div 3 = 3)}2$

2. $\frac{6}{2} = \frac{}{2} + \frac{}{2} + \frac{}{2} = $ ___
   $\frac{6}{2} = $ __ + __ + __ = __

   $\frac{6}{2} = 6 \div$ __ $= \overline{)} = $ __

3. $\frac{7}{2} = $ ___ + ___ + ___ + ___ = ___
   $\frac{7}{2} = $ ___ + ___ + ___ + ___ = ___

   $\frac{7}{2} = $ __ $\div$ __ $= \overline{)} = $ __

4. $\frac{9}{4} = $ ___ + ___ + ___ = ___
   $\frac{9}{4} = $ ___ + ___ + ___ = ___

   $\frac{9}{4} = $ __ $\div$ __ $= \overline{)} = $ __

5. $\frac{7}{3} = $ ___ + ___ + ___ = ___
   $\frac{7}{3} = $ ___ + ___ + ___ = ___

   $\frac{7}{3} = $ __ $\div$ __ $= \overline{)} = $ __

6. $\frac{9}{8} = $ ___ + ___ = ___
   $\frac{9}{8} = $ ___ + ___ = ___

   $\frac{9}{8} = $ __ $\div$ __ $= \overline{)} = $ __

7. $\frac{17}{8} = $ ___ + ___ + ___ = ___
   $\frac{17}{8} = $ ___ + ___ + ___ = ___

   $\frac{17}{8} = $ __ $\div$ __ $= \overline{)} = $ __

Complete the following. Show your work.

8. $\frac{11}{6} = $

9. $\frac{15}{9} = $

10. $\frac{8}{5} = $

Name _____   Date _____

Learning to Add Fractions With Like Denominators

Complete the following problems. Simplify the answers.

1. $\frac{5}{8}$
   $+\frac{1}{8}$

2. $\frac{7}{8}$
   $+\frac{3}{8}$

3. $\frac{11}{16}$
   $+\frac{4}{16}$

4. $\frac{3}{4}$
   $+\frac{1}{4}$

5. $\frac{7}{12}$
   $+\frac{2}{12}$

6. $\frac{8}{11}$
   $+\frac{2}{11}$

7. $\frac{7}{10}$
   $+\frac{2}{10}$

8. $\frac{3}{5}$
   $+\frac{1}{5}$

Learning to Add Fractions With Unlike Denominators

Complete the following problems. The first one has been done for you. Simplify the answers.

9. $\frac{2}{3} \times \frac{2}{2} = \frac{4}{6}$
   $+ \frac{1}{2} \times \frac{3}{3} = \frac{3}{6}$
   $\qquad\qquad \frac{7}{6} = 1\frac{1}{6}$

10. $\frac{1}{2} \times$ ___ = ___
   $+ \frac{3}{8} \times$ ___ = ___

11. $\frac{3}{4} \times$ ___ = ___
   $+ \frac{1}{3} \times$ ___ = ___

12. $\frac{3}{8} \times$ ___ = ___
   $+ \frac{1}{2} \times$ ___ = ___

13. $\frac{3}{5} \times$ ___ = ___
   $+ \frac{2}{3} \times$ ___ = ___

14. $\frac{1}{4} \times$ ___ = ___
   $+ \frac{1}{3} \times$ ___ = ___

15. $\frac{5}{8} \times$ ___ = ___
   $+ \frac{1}{4} \times$ ___ = ___

16. $\frac{5}{9} \times$ ___ = ___
   $+ \frac{2}{3} \times$ ___ = ___

17. $\frac{5}{12} \times$ ___ = ___
   $+ \frac{1}{3} \times$ ___ = ___

18. $\frac{6}{7}$
   $+\frac{1}{2}$

19. $\frac{7}{10}$
   $+\frac{2}{5}$

20. $\frac{7}{9}$
   $+\frac{1}{3}$

Name _____   Date _____

 Learning to Subtract Fractions With Like Denominators

Complete the following problems. Simplify the answers.

1. $\frac{5}{8}$ 2. $\frac{7}{8}$ 3. $\frac{11}{16}$ 4. $\frac{3}{4}$
  $-\frac{1}{8}$ $-\frac{3}{8}$ $-\frac{4}{16}$ $-\frac{1}{4}$

5. $\frac{7}{12}$ 6. $\frac{8}{11}$ 7. $\frac{7}{10}$ 8. $\frac{3}{5}$
  $-\frac{2}{12}$ $-\frac{2}{11}$ $-\frac{2}{10}$ $-\frac{1}{5}$

 Learning to Subtract Fractions With Unlike Denominators

Complete the following problems. The first one has been done for you. Simplify the answers.

9. $\frac{2}{3}$ x $\frac{2}{2}$ = $\frac{4}{6}$ 10. $\frac{1}{2}$ x ___ = ___   11. $\frac{3}{4}$ x ___ = ___
  $-\frac{1}{2}$ x $\frac{3}{3}$ = $\frac{3}{6}$ $-\frac{3}{8}$ x ___ = ___ $-\frac{1}{3}$ x ___ = ___
                    $\frac{1}{6}$

12. $\frac{1}{2}$ x ___ = ___   13. $\frac{2}{3}$ x ___ = ___   14. $\frac{1}{3}$ x ___ = ___
   $-\frac{3}{8}$ x ___ = ___ $-\frac{3}{5}$ x ___ = ___ $-\frac{1}{4}$ x ___ = ___

15. $\frac{5}{8}$ x ___ = ___   16. $\frac{2}{3}$ x ___ = ___   17. $\frac{5}{12}$ x ___ = ___
   $-\frac{1}{4}$ x ___ = ___ $-\frac{5}{9}$ x ___ = ___ $+\frac{1}{3}$ x ___ = ___

18. $\frac{6}{7}$ 19. $\frac{7}{10}$ 20. $\frac{7}{9}$
  $-\frac{1}{2}$ $-\frac{2}{5}$ $-\frac{1}{3}$

Name _____ Date _____

Learning to Add Improper Fractions

Complete the following problems. The first one is done for you. Simplify the answers.

1. $\frac{5}{2}$
   $+\frac{3}{2}$
   $\frac{8}{2}=2\overline{)8}=4$
   $\underline{8}$
   0

2. $\frac{7}{4}$
   $+\frac{5}{4}$

3. $\frac{5}{3}$
   $+\frac{4}{3}$

4. $\frac{11}{8}$
   $+\frac{9}{8}$

5. $\frac{7}{3}$
   $+\frac{5}{3}$

6. $\frac{8}{5}$
   $+\frac{6}{5}$

7. $\frac{6}{4}$
   $+\frac{5}{4}$

8. $\frac{9}{8}$
   $+\frac{9}{8}$

9. $\frac{11}{10}$
   $+\frac{10}{10}$

Reviewing Addition and Subtraction of Fractions

Change the following improper fractions to mixed numbers. The first one has been done for you. Simplify the answers.

1. $\frac{12}{8}=2\overline{)12}=1\frac{4}{8}=1\frac{1}{2}$ 2. $\frac{5}{3}$
   $\underline{8}$
   4

3. $\frac{10}{3}$

4. $\frac{8}{6}$

Change the following mixed numbers to improper fractions. The first one has been done for you.

5. $1\frac{3}{4}=(4 \times 1) + 3 =\frac{7}{4}$ 6. $3\frac{1}{3}$

7. $2\frac{3}{4}$

8. $5\frac{1}{8}$

Add or Subtract. Simplify the answers.

9. $\frac{5}{8}$
   $-\frac{3}{8}$

10. $\frac{6}{7}$
    $+\frac{1}{7}$

11. $\frac{7}{9}$
    $-\frac{1}{9}$

12. $\frac{3}{4}$
    $+\frac{1}{4}$

Add the following improper fractions. Change the answer to a mixed number and simplify the fractions.

13. $\frac{9}{5}$
    $+\frac{4}{5}$

14. $\frac{6}{4}$
    $+\frac{5}{3}$

15. $\frac{3}{2}$
    $+\frac{3}{4}$

16. $\frac{4}{3}$
    $+\frac{3}{2}$

Name _____   Date _____

$125 + 300 = 425$ $750 - 400 = 350$ $5 \times (3 \times 7) = 3 \times (5 \times 7)$ $3/4 - 1/4 = 1/2$
$5 \times (3 \times 7) = 3 \times (3 \times 7)$ $3/4 - 1/4 = 1/2$ $125 + 300 = 425$ $750 - 400 = 350$

Learning About Multiplying Fractions

Whole Numbers Times Fractions

Solve the following multiplication problems. The first one has been completed. Simplify the answers.

1. $5 \times \frac{1}{3} = \frac{5}{1} \times \frac{1}{3} \times \frac{5}{3} = 3\overline{)5}^{\;1} = 1\frac{2}{3}$
$\phantom{1. 5 \times \frac{1}{3} = }\begin{array}{r}3\\2\end{array}$

2. $4 \times \frac{2}{3} = $ ___ $\times$ ___ $=$ ___ $= \overline{)} = $ ___

3. $8 \times \frac{3}{4} = $

4. $6 \times \frac{1}{2} = $

5. $8 \times \frac{2}{3} = $

6. $12 \times \frac{3}{4} = $

7. $9 \times \frac{2}{5} = $

8. $6 \times \frac{1}{5} = $

9. $3 \times \frac{3}{4} = $

10. $7 \times \frac{1}{6} = $

Fractions Times Whole Numbers

Solve the following multiplication problems. The first one has been completed. Simplify the answers.

1. Find $\frac{3}{4}$ of 12. $\frac{3}{4} \times \frac{12}{1} = \frac{36}{4} = 4\overline{)36}^{\;9} = 9$

2. Find $\frac{1}{3}$ of 12. $\frac{1}{3} \times \frac{12}{1} = $ ___ $= \overline{)} = $ ___

3. Find $\frac{2}{5}$ of 25.

4. Find $\frac{2}{3}$ of 10.

5. Find $\frac{3}{8}$ of 9.

6. Find $\frac{2}{7}$ of 14.

7. Find $\frac{5}{6}$ of 12.

8. Find $\frac{1}{8}$ of 12.

9. Find $\frac{3}{5}$ of 15.

10. Find $\frac{3}{4}$ of 6.

Name _____ Date _____

Multiplying Fractions Times Fractions

Solve the following multiplication problems.

1. $\frac{1}{3}$ x $\frac{1}{2}$ = _____

2. $\frac{3}{4}$ x $\frac{1}{3}$ = _____

3. $\frac{3}{4}$ x $\frac{2}{3}$ = _____

4. $\frac{1}{5}$ x $\frac{1}{3}$ = _____

5. $\frac{3}{5}$ x $\frac{1}{2}$ = _____

6. $\frac{2}{3}$ x $\frac{4}{5}$ = _____

7. $\frac{3}{10}$ x $\frac{1}{4}$ = _____

8. $\frac{6}{7}$ x $\frac{2}{5}$ = _____

9. $\frac{3}{8}$ x $\frac{2}{3}$ = _____

10. $\frac{4}{5}$ x $\frac{1}{2}$ = _____

11. $\frac{5}{8}$ x $\frac{1}{3}$ = _____

12. $\frac{7}{8}$ x $\frac{2}{9}$ = _____

Multiplying Mixed Numbers

Solve the following multiplication problems. Change the mixed numbers to improper fractions then multiply numerator times numerator and denominator times denominator. Change answers to mixed numbers. Simplify all fraction answers. The first one has been completed.

1. $1\frac{1}{2}$ x $1\frac{2}{3}$ = $\frac{3}{2}$ x $\frac{5}{3}$ = $\frac{15}{6}$ = $2\frac{3}{15}$ or $2\frac{1}{5}$

2. $1\frac{2}{3}$ x $2\frac{1}{3}$ = _____ x _____ = _____ = _____ or ___ _____

3. $2\frac{2}{3}$ x $1\frac{5}{8}$ = _____ x _____ = _____ = _____ or ___ _____

4. $3\frac{1}{3}$ x $1\frac{1}{3}$ = _____ x _____ = _____ = _____ or ___ _____

5. $1\frac{1}{5}$ x $1\frac{1}{2}$ = _____ x _____ = _____ = _____ or ___ _____

6. $3\frac{1}{3}$ x $2\frac{1}{2}$ = _____ x _____ = _____ = _____ or ___ _____

7. $1\frac{1}{5}$ x $1\frac{3}{4}$ = _____ x _____ = _____ = _____ or ___ _____

8. $5\frac{1}{3}$ x $1\frac{1}{3}$ = _____ x _____ = _____ = _____ or ___ _____

9. $1\frac{2}{5}$ x $1\frac{1}{2}$ = _____ x _____ = _____ = _____ or ___ _____

10. $1\frac{2}{5}$ x $6\frac{1}{2}$ = _____ x _____ = _____ = _____ or ___ _____

Name _____ Date _____

Learning About Dividing Fractions

Solve the following division problems with fractions. Simplify fraction answers. Check each answer. The first one has been completed.

1. $\frac{3}{7} \div \frac{1}{3} = \frac{3}{7} \times \frac{3}{1} = \frac{9}{7} = 1\frac{2}{7}$

Check: $\frac{9}{7} \times \frac{1}{3} = \frac{9}{21} = \frac{3}{7}$

2. $\frac{2}{5} \div \frac{1}{2} =$ ___ x ___ = ___ = ___

Check: ___ x ___ = ___ = ___

3. $\frac{3}{4} \div \frac{1}{4} =$ ___ x ___ = ___ = ___

Check: ___ x ___ = ___ = ___

4. $\frac{1}{8} \div \frac{1}{2} =$ ___ x ___ = ___ = ___

Check: ___ x ___ = ___ = ___

5. $\frac{2}{3} \div \frac{1}{3} =$ ___ x ___ = ___ = ___

Check: ___ x ___ = ___ = ___

6. $\frac{5}{8} \div \frac{1}{4} =$ ___ x ___ = ___ = ___

Check: ___ x ___ = ___ = ___

7. $\frac{3}{10} \div \frac{1}{2} =$ ___ x ___ = ___ = ___

Check: ___ x ___ = ___ = ___

8. $\frac{2}{3} \div \frac{6}{7} =$ ___ x ___ = ___ = ___

Check: ___ x ___ = ___ = ___

9. $\frac{2}{3} \div \frac{2}{7} =$ ___ x ___ = ___ = ___

Check: ___ x ___ = ___ = ___

10. $\frac{5}{9} \div \frac{1}{4} =$ ___ x ___ = ___ = ___

Check: ___ x ___ = ___ = ___

11. $\frac{3}{10} \div \frac{1}{3} =$ ___ x ___ = ___ = ___

Check: ___ x ___ = ___ = ___

12. $\frac{3}{4} \div \frac{6}{7} =$ ___ x ___ = ___ = ___

Check: ___ x ___ = ___ = ___

Name _____   Date _____

 Writing a Decimal for a Statement

Change the following fractions to decimals. The first one has been completed.

1. $\frac{3}{5}$ = 5$\overline{)3.0}$ = 5$\overline{)\overset{.6}{3.0}}$ = 0.6 or 0.60 or 0.600
                              3.0

2. $\frac{3}{4}$

3. $\frac{5}{6}$

4. $\frac{1}{2}$

5. $\frac{1}{4}$

6. $\frac{5}{8}$

Write the number on the blank for each statement. Remember the decimal point.

7. One and six tenths _____

8. Eight hundredths _____

9. Seven and one tenth _____

10. Seven and ten hundredths _____

11. One hundred seven and sixty-seven hundredths _____

12. Four hundred thirty-two and seven thousandths _____

13. Fifty-six thousandths _____

14. One thousand seventy-three and four tenths _____

15. Three thousandths _____

16. Three and ninety-nine hundredths _____

Name _____   Date _____

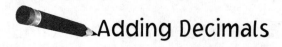

Adding Decimals

Add the following decimals. Remember to keep the decimal points in a line.

17.   0.34
     + 0.03

18. 1.34 + 0.234 + 0.012 + 24.45 = _____

19. 234.90 + 1567.09 + 1.56 + 0.008 = _____

Subtracting Decimals

20. 0.34	21. 23.8	22. 45.89	23. 2.56	24. 45.67
- 0.03	- 12.4	- 0.98	- 0.05	- 36.57

Multiplying Decimals

25. 34.5	26. 0.45	27. 3.78	28. 0.67	29. 45.67
x 0.3	x 0.05	x 0.23	x 0.8	x 36.57

Dividing Decimals

30. 6)‾2.4   31. 24)‾4.80   32. 0.6)‾2.4   33. 15)‾31.5

$125 + 300 = 425$ $750 - $██$0 = 350$ $5 \times (3 \times 7) = 3 \times (5 \times 7)$ $3/4 - 1/4 = 1/2$
$5 \times (3 \times 7) = 3 \times (5 \times 7)$ $3/4 - $██ Answer Key ██$00 = 425$ $750 - 400 = 350$

Assessment for Place Value–p. 3-5

1. 10, 2
2. 10, 8
3. 10, 10, 5
4. 10, 10, 10, 10, 10, 10, 10, 10, 4
5. 10, 10, 10, 10, 10, 10, 10, 10, 10, 8
6. 1, 2
7. 1, 8
8. 2, 5
9. 8, 4
10. 9, 8
11. 13
12. 14
13. 73
14. 88
15. 99
16. 83
17. 66
18. 20
19. 80
20. 50
21. 71
22. 80, 8
23. 30, 6
24. 40, 0
25. 90, 7
26. 2, 3
27. 4, 7
28. 7, 8
29. 9, 0
30. 3, 0
31. 8, 7
32. 3, 8
33. 6, 3
34. 9, 6
35. 7, 0
36. 56
37. 7, 4
38. d
39. a. seventy
    b. thirty
    c. eight
    d. ten
    e. fifty
40. a. ten
    b. ten
    c. ten
    d. ten
    e. ten

41. a. 50, 2
    b. 90, 2
    c. 80, 7
    d. 90, 9
    e. 10, 2
42. a. 9
    b. 64
    c. 125
    d. 32
    e. 3,125
43. a. 2^2
    b. 3^2
    c. 8^2 or 4^3 or 2^6
    d. 2^4 or 4^2
    e. 3^3
    f. 6^3

Assessment for Addition Activities p. 7

1. 11
2. 17
3. 13
4. 11
5. 14
6. 8
7. 23
8. 19
9. 36
10. 82
11. 90
12. 85
13. 147
14. 181
15. 238
16. 242
17. 549
18. 679
19. 682
20. 905
21. 517
22. 1,130
23. 912
24. 1,613

Assessment for Subtraction Activities-p. 9

1. 7
2. 9
3. 1
4. 6
5. 21

6. 41
7. 10
8. 24
9. 31
10. 13
11. 61
12. 10
13. 16
14. 9
15. 19
16. 9
17. 109
18. 92
19. 1,910
20. 889
21. 9
22. 9
23. 189
24. 89
25. 889

Assessment for Multiplication-Part I- p. 11

1. 2
2. 4
3. 6
4. 8
5. 10
6. 12
7. 14
8. 16
9. 18
10. 20
11. 22
12. 24
13. 3
14. 6
15. 9
16. 12
17. 15
18. 18
19. 21
20. 24
21. 27
22. 30
23. 33
24. 36
25. 4
26. 8
27. 12
28. 16

29. 20
30. 24
31. 28
32. 32
33. 36
34. 40
35. 44
36. 48
37. 5
38. 10
39. 15
40. 20
41. 25
42. 30
43. 35
44. 40
45. 45
46. 50
47. 55
48. 60
49. 6
50. 12
51. 18
52. 24
53. 30
54. 36
55. 42
56. 48
57. 54
58. 60
59. 66
60. 72
61. 7
62. 14
63. 21
64. 28
65. 35
66. 42
67. 49
68. 56
69. 63
70. 70
71. 77
72. 84
73. 8
74. 16
75. 24
76. 32
77. 40
78. 48
79. 56
80. 64

81. 72
82. 80
83. 88
84. 96
85. 9
86. 18
87. 27
88. 36
89. 45
90. 54
91. 63
92. 72
93. 81
94. 90
95. 99
96. 108
97. 10
98. 20
99. 30
100. 40
101. 50
102. 60
103. 70
104. 80
105. 90
106. 100
107. 110
108. 120
109. 11
110. 22
111. 33
112. 44
113. 55
114. 66
115. 77
116. 88
117. 99
118. 110
119. 121
120. 132

Assessment for Multiplication—Part II-p. 12

1. 28
2. 72
3. 60
4. 28
5. 270
6. 408
7. 186
8. 189

Assessment for Multiplication—Part III-p. 12

1. 15, 120

2. 12, 24
3. 8, 80
4. 54, 5, 270
5. 10, 27, 270
6. 35, 20, 700
7. 560, 4, 2,240
8. 30, 10, 300
9. 48, 20, 960

Assessment for Multiplication—Part IV-p. 12

1. 100, 40, 140
2. 30, 5, 30, 5, 180, 30, 210
3. 8, 80, 9, 80, 9, 640, 72, 712
4. 7, 300, 40, 300, 40, 2100, 280, 2380

5. 4, 500, 40, 8, 500, 40, 8, 2000, 160, 32, 2192

Assessment for Multiplication—Part V-p. 12

1. 70
2. 272
3. 840
4. 4,224
5. 14,742
6. 29,280
7. 237,489
8. 1,020,075

Assessment for Division—Part I-p. 13

1. 5
2. 2
3. 3
4. 4
5. 2
6. 15
7. 9
8. 24
9. 3
10. 8
11. 6
12. 11
13. 24
14. 3
15. 7
16. 40
17. 31
18. 44

19. 259
20. 47
21. 21
22. 105
23. 110
24. 70

Assessment for Division—Part II-p. 14

1. 6
2. 7
3. 22
4. 27
5. 22
6. 40
7. 21
8. 39
9. 23
10. 25
11. 8
12. 4
13. 23
14. 44
15. 50
16. 49
17. 1r5
18. 4
19. 7r40
20. 7r12
21. 23
22. 12
23. 2r351
24. 35r5

Assessment for Fractions-p. 15-17

1. $\frac{1}{3}$
2. $\frac{3}{4}$
3. $\frac{1}{2}$
4. $\frac{3}{5}$
5. $\frac{2}{3}$
6.-9. Teacher check diagram.
10. $\frac{1}{2}, \frac{1}{3}, \frac{1}{4}, \frac{1}{6}, \frac{1}{8}, \frac{1}{16}$
11. 1, 1, 1, 1, 1, 9
12. 8, 2, 3, 4, 6, 16, 4, 16, 8, 16
13. $\frac{2}{4}, \frac{4}{8}, \frac{8}{16}$
14. None equal one-fourth
15. $\frac{12}{16}, \frac{24}{32}, \frac{3}{4}$
16. None equal one-sixteenth
17. a
18. b
19. c

20. d
21. a. $\frac{4}{4}$ or 1
    b. $\frac{7}{8}$
    c. $\frac{9}{16}$
    d. $\frac{5}{8}$
    e. $\frac{7}{8}$
22. a. $\frac{1}{8}$
    b. $\frac{2}{6}$ or $\frac{1}{3}$
    c. $\frac{3}{16}$
    d. $\frac{1}{6}$
    e. $\frac{7}{16}$
23. a. $\frac{2}{9}$
    b. $\frac{3}{16}$
    c. $\frac{6}{15}$ or $\frac{2}{5}$
24. a. $\frac{3}{6}$ or $\frac{1}{2}$
    b. $\frac{6}{8}$ or $\frac{3}{4}$
    c. $\frac{9}{10}$
25. $\frac{7}{6}, \frac{3}{2}, \frac{9}{8}, \frac{5}{4}, \frac{4}{3}$
26. a. $1\frac{7}{8}, 3\frac{1}{2}, 2\frac{2}{3}$
    b. $5\frac{3}{4}, 3\frac{3}{5}$
27. a. $\frac{5}{3}$
    b. $\frac{7}{2}$
    c. $\frac{11}{4}$
28. a. $1\frac{1}{6}$
    b. $1\frac{4}{5}$
    c. $1\frac{7}{9}$
29. a. $\frac{9}{3} = 3$
    b. $\frac{7}{2} = 3\frac{1}{2}$
    c. $\frac{8}{6} = 1\frac{1}{3}$
30. a. $\frac{1}{3}$
    b. $\frac{2}{5}$
    c. 0
31. a. $\frac{15}{4} = 3\frac{3}{4}$
    b. $\frac{10}{9} = 1\frac{1}{9}$
    c. $\frac{15}{6} = 2\frac{1}{2}$

Assessment for Decimals-p. 18

1. 0.3
2. 0.05
3. 0.35
4. 0.005
5. 0.165
6. 0.6
7. 0.05
8. 1.5
9. 2.45
10. 0.003
11. 0.126
12. 0.50
13. 0.75
14. 0.4

Learning About Place Value-p. 53

1. 56
2. 81

3. Answers may vary.
4. c
5. c
6. a
7. Teacher check

Understanding More About Place Value-p. 54

1. 1, 4
2. 1, 0
3. 7, 3
4. 8, 9
5. 1, 2, 3
6. 3, 4, 5
7. 9, 0, 8
8. 1, 3, 5, 6
9. 7, 6, 5, 4
10. 9, 0, 4, 5

Improving in Understanding of Place Value-p. 54

1. 7, 1
2. 700, 100
3. 6, 6
4. 60, 60
5. 1, 7
6. 1, 7

Understanding Expanded Notation-p. 55

1. $(4 \times 100) + (8 \times 10) + (6 \times 1)$
2. $(17 \times 100) + (8 \times 10) + (6 \times 1)$
3. $(1 \times 1,000) + (9 \times 100) + (2 \times 10) + (3 \times 1)$
4. $(2 \times 1,000) + (5 \times 100) + (4 \times 10) + (3 \times 1)$
5. $(1 \times 100) + (2 \times 10) + (4 \times 1)$
6. $(2 \times 100) + (4 \times 10) + (1 \times 1)$
7. $(4 \times 100) + (2 \times 10) + (1 \times 1)$
8. $(1 \times 10) + (2 \times 1)$
9. $(2 \times 10) + (1 \times 1)$
10. $(4 \times 100) + (0 \times 10) + (1 \times 1)$
11. $(1 \times 100) + (4 \times 10) + (0 \times 1)$
12. $(5 \times 10) + (4 \times 1)$
13. $(7 \times 100) + (4 \times 10)$

$+ (3 \times 1)$
14. $(2 \times 1,000) + (6 \times 100) + (7 \times 10) + (5 \times 1)$

Learning About Exponents-p. 56

1. $2, ^1, 2^1$
2. $2, ^2, 2^2$
3. $2, ^3, 2^3$
4. $2, ^4, 2^4$ or $4, ^2, 4^2$
5. $2, ^5, 2^5$
6. $2, ^6, 2^6$ or $4, ^3, 4^3$ or $8, ^2, 8^2$
7. 1
8. 10
9. 100
10. 1,000
11. 10,000
12. 100,000
13. 1,000,000
14. 10,000,000
15. 100,000,000

Exponent Practice-p. 57

1. $27, 3^3$
2. $16, 4^2$
3. $100,000, 10^5$
4. $128, 2^7$
5. $1,296, 6^4$
6. $512, 8^3$
7. $121, 11^2$
8. $248,832, 12^5$
9. $4,096, 4^6$
10. $3,125, 5^5$
11. 8
12. 6^2
13. 5
14. 2
15. 5
16. 1
17. 4
18. $10, ^5$
19. 10^2
20. 2^4
21. 3^7
22. Multiply

Learning About Base Five and Base Ten-p. 58

1. 1, 2, 3, 4, 10, 11, 12, 13, 14, 20, 21, 22, 23, 24, 30, 31, 32, 33, 34, 40, 41, 42, 43, 44, 100

2. $(1 \times 25) + (2 \times 5) + (3 \times 1) = 38_{10}$
3. $(1 \times 25) + (2 \times 5) + (4 \times 1) = 39_{10}$
4. $(1 \times 25) + (2 \times 5) + (2 \times 1) = 37_{10}$
5. $(2 \times 25) + (1 \times 5) + (1 \times 1) = 56_{10}$
6. $(3 \times 25) + (0 \times 5) + (1 \times 1) = 76_{10}$
7. $(3 \times 25) + (1 \times 5) + (2 \times 1) = 82_{10}$
8. $(4 \times 25) + (2 \times 5) + (2 \times 1) = 112_{10}$
9. $(1 \times 25) + (1 \times 5) + (1 \times 1) = 31_{10}$
10. $(2 \times 125) + (2 \times 25) + (2 \times 5) + (2 \times 1) = 312_{10}$

Review Lessons-p. 59-60

1. 653
2. 4,304
3. 8
4. 4
5. a. 326
   b. 5,936
   c. 2,042
   d. 9,000
6. a. 10^3
   b. 2^4
   c. 5^2
   d. 3^5
   e. 4^3
7. a. 16
   b. 49
   c. 64
   d. 1,000
   e. 625
8. a. $(1 \times 25) + (1 \times 5) + (1 \times 1) = 31_{10}$
   b. $(1 \times 25) + (1 \times 5) + (0 \times 1) = 30_{10}$
   c. $(1 \times 25) + (0 \times 5) + (1 \times 1) = 26_{10}$
   d. $(2 \times 25) + (3 \times 5) + (2 \times 1) = 67_{10}$
   e. $(3 \times 25) + (1 \times 5) + (1 \times 1) = 81_{10}$
   f. $(2 \times 25) + (0 \times 5) + (1 \times 1) = 51_{10}$
   g. $(2 \times 25) + (2 \times 5) + (2 \times 1) = 62_{10}$
   h. $(1 \times 25) + (4 \times 5) + (4 \times 1) = 49_{10}$
   i. $(1 \times 125) + (4 \times$

$25) + (2 \times 5) + (3 \times 1) = 238_{10}$
9. a. 6_{10}
   b. 7_{10}
   c. 74_{10}
   d. 18_{10}
   e. 38_{10}

Checking Understanding of Addition-p. 61

1. 5, 4, 50, 4
   3, 2, 30, 2
   86, 8, 6, 80, 6
2. 6, 2, 60, 2
   2, 7, 20, 7
   89, 8, 9, 80, 9
3. 8, 5, 80, 5
   1, 4, 10, 4
   99, 9, 9, 90, 9
4. 0, 9, 0, 9
   0, 9, 0, 9
   18, 1, 8, 10, 8
5. 8, 8, 80, 8
   1, 1, 10, 1
   99, 9, 9, 90, 9
6. 1, 2, 4, 100, 20, 4
   1, 6, 4, 100, 60, 4
   288, 2, 8, 8, 200, 80, 8
7. 4, 5, 6, 400, 50, 6
   3, 4, 2, 300, 40, 2
   798, 7, 9, 8, 700, 90, 8

Checking Skills in Regrouping-p. 62

1. 7, 8, 78,
   1, 3, 13,
   8, 11, 91
2. 0, 6, 7, 67,
   0, 4, 7, 47,
   0, 10, 14, 114
3. 582
4. 813
5. 1,020
6. 1,021
7. 1,000
8. 57
9. 62
10. 92
11. 998
12. 1,000
13. 1,002
14. 1,004
15. 1,006
16. 1,008

17. yes
18. yes
19. yes

More Addition Practice-p. 63

1. 34
2. 79
3. 51
4. 88
5. 39
6. 95
7. 163
8. 147
9. 420
10. 536
11. 953
12. 379
13. 751
14. 1,023
15. 1,085
16. 1,059
17. 141
18. 204
19. 1,587
20. 1,686

Learning About Subtraction-p. 64

1. 5, 4, 50, 4,
   3, 2, 30, 2,
   22, 2, 2, 20, 2
2. 6, 2, 60,
   2, 2, 1, 20, 1,
   41, 4, 1, 40, 1
3. 8, 5, 80, 5,
   1, 4, 10, 4,
   71, 7, 1, 70, 1
4. 0, 9, 0, 9,
   0, 9, 0, 9,
   0, 0, 0, 0, 0
5. 8, 8, 80, 8,
   1, 1, 10, 1,
   77, 7, 7, 70, 7
6. 1, 6, 4, 100, 60, 4,
   1, 2, 4, 100, 20, 4,
   40, 0, 4, 0, 40, 0
7. 4, 5, 6, 400, 50, 6,
   3, 4, 2, 300, 40, 2,
   114, 1, 1, 4, 100,
   10, 4

Checking Skills in Regrouping-p. 65-66

1. 70 + 8; 10 + 9; 60 +
   18; -10 + 9; 50 + 9;

59, 59, 59, 19
2. 60 + 7; 40 + 8; 50 +
   17; -40 + 8; 10 + 9;
   19, 19, 48, 19
3. 80 + 6; 60 + 7; 70 +
   16; -60 + 7; 10 + 9;
   19, 19, 67, 19, 86
4. 110; 110, 236
5. 375; 375, 219, 594
6. 336; 336, 342, 678
7. 90; 90, 786, 876
8. 189; 189, 789, 978
9. 43
10. 67
11. 89

More Subtraction Practice-p. 67

1. 12
2. 13
3. 21
4. 20
5. 9
6. 19
7. 9
8. 9
9. 136
10. 110
11. 21
12. 11
13. 78
14. 178
15. 118
16. 93

Addition and Subtraction Practice-p. 67

1. sum
2. sum
3. difference
4. difference
5. 71
6. 135
7. 992
8. 1,091
9. 89
10. 1,421
11. 888
12. 10,619

Learning About Multiplication-p. 68 The Associative Property

1. 15, 30
2. 20, 20

3. 32, 40
4. 21, 27
5. 24, 120
6. 350, 4, 14, 100
7. 525, 30, 35, 450
8. 8, 200, 400, 4
9. 168, 5, 7, 120
10. 52, 60, 624, 5
11. 720
12. 40, 18, 720
13. 4,320
14. 48, 90, 4,320
15. 11,250
16. 225, 50, 11,250
17. 43,470
18. 161, 270, 43,470
19. 26,784
20. 279, 96, 26,784

Multiplication: The Distributive Property-p. 69

1. 20, 24, 44
2. 160, 32, 192
3. 7, 7, 7, 210, 42, 252
4. 3, 3, 3, 3, 3, 8, 9,
   24, 33
5. 7, 10, 21, 30, 51
6. 5, 30, 8, 150, 540,
   190
7. 70, 8, 70, 8, 5, 560,
   40, 600
8. 12, 12, 100, 12, 20,
   1,200, 240, 1,440
9. 25, 100, 25, 100,
   25, 50, 2,500,
   1,250, 3,750
10. 85, 9, 85, 60, 85, 9,
    5,100, 765, 5,865

Multiplication Practice-p. 69

1. 69
2. 1,284
3. 462
4. 9,999
5. 62
6. 868
7. 9,333
8. 9,876
9. 128
10. 1,869
11. 15,969
12. 2,888

Developing Regrouping Skills-p. 69

1. 215
2. 4,458
3. 51,448
4. 78,687
5. 536
6. 5,978
7. 6,342
8. 34,584
9. 400
10. 4,856
11. 12,021
12. 45,360

Regrouping Using Larger Numbers-p. 70

1. 714
2. 704
3. 1,608
4. 5,240
5. 1,166
6. 13,563
7. 53,326
8. 36,663
9. 1,088
10. 3,445
11. 3,120
12. 5,568
13. 4,148
14. 2,136
15. 3,996
16. 3,366
17. 10,395
18. 33,744
19. 21,735
20. 42,174
21. 50,076
22. 16,984
23. 194,480
24. 660,436

Checking Understanding of Division-p. 71

1. 3
2. 2
3. 2
4. 3
5. 6
6. 5
7. 3
8. 5
9. 9
10. 4
11. 6
12. 6
13. 8
14. 8

15. 9
16. 9
17. 9
18. 6
19. 9
20. 22

Understanding Division With Remainders-p. 72

1. 7r1
2. 5r2
3. 5r2
4. 4r4
5. 4r1
6. 9r2
7. 6r3
8. 23r2
9. 4r2
10. 15r4
11. 8r3
12. 11r8

One- and Two-Digit Divisors Without Remainders-p. 72

1. 23
2. 21
3. 18
4. 11
5. 18
6. 37
7. 43
8. 81
9. 5
10. 3
11. 11
12. 12
13. 9
14. 28
15. 23
16. 22

Two-Digit Divisors With Remainders-p. 73

1. 19r4
2. 6r40
3. 26r3
4. 5r55
5. 14r7
6. 66r7
7. 67r13
8. 5r7
9. 34r7
10. 37r14
11. 21r7
12. 8r50

13. 6r1
14. 7r29
15. 21r11
16. 38r2
17. 38r5
18. 14r9
19. 1r36
20. 22r13
21. 23r1
22. 28r13
23. 8r34
24. 22r20

Learning About Simple Fractions-p. 74-77

1. $\frac{1}{2}$
2. $\frac{1}{4}$
3. $\frac{1}{8}$
4.-7. Teacher check
8. 128, $\frac{1}{128}$
9. Teacher check, $\frac{1}{32}$
10. $\frac{1}{2}$
11. $\frac{1}{4}$
12. $\frac{1}{8}$
13. $\frac{1}{16}$
14. $\frac{1}{32}$
15. $\frac{1}{2}$, $\frac{1}{4}$, $\frac{1}{8}$, $\frac{1}{16}$, $\frac{1}{32}$
16. True
17. a.-g. Teacher check
18. 2
19. 4
20. 8
21. 16
22. 2
23. 4
24. 8
25. 2
26. 6
27. 12
28. 24
29. 6
30. 10
31. 10
32. $\frac{2}{8}$, $\frac{4}{16}$, $\frac{8}{32}$
33. $\frac{4}{8}$, $\frac{8}{16}$, $\frac{16}{32}$
34. $\frac{6}{8}$, $\frac{9}{12}$, $\frac{24}{32}$

Learning About Equivalent Fractions-p. 78

1. $\frac{3}{24}$
2. $\frac{2}{16}$
3. $\frac{4}{32}$
4. $\frac{4}{8}$
5. $\frac{3}{6}$
6. $\frac{2}{4}$

7. $\frac{2}{8}$
8. $\frac{3}{12}$
9. $\frac{5}{20}$
10. $\frac{3}{9}$
11. $\frac{4}{12}$
12. $\frac{2}{6}$
13. $\frac{6}{8}$
14. $\frac{8}{12}$
15. $\frac{9}{24}$
16. $\frac{10}{16}$
17. $\frac{9}{30}$
18. $\frac{8}{16}$
19. $\frac{2}{32}$
20. $\frac{28}{8}$
21. $\frac{6}{10}$
22. $\frac{20}{24}$
23. $\frac{4}{10}$
24. $\frac{9}{12}$
25.-46. Answers will vary.
47. a. $\frac{1}{2}$
    b. $\frac{1}{3}$
    c. $\frac{1}{4}$
    d. $\frac{1}{5}$
    e. $\frac{1}{6}$
    f. $\frac{1}{8}$
    g. $\frac{1}{9}$
    h. $\frac{1}{10}$
    i. $\frac{1}{12}$
    j. $\frac{1}{16}$

Reviewing Fractions-p. 79

1.-12. Teacher check
13. greater
14. greater
15. greater
16. less
17. less
18. less
19. less
20. less
21. greater
22. greater
23. less
24. greater

Learning About Improper Fractions-p. 80

Teacher: Check work on this section.

1. $2\frac{2}{3}$
2. 3
3. $3\frac{1}{2}$
4. $2\frac{1}{4}$
5. $2\frac{1}{3}$

6. $1\frac{1}{8}$
7. $2\frac{1}{8}$
8. $1\frac{5}{6}$
9. $1\frac{6}{9}$ or $1\frac{2}{3}$
10. $1\frac{3}{5}$

Learning to Add Fractions-p. 81

1. $\frac{6}{8} = \frac{3}{4}$
2. $1\frac{2}{8} = 1\frac{1}{4}$
3. $\frac{15}{16}$
4. 1
5. $\frac{9}{12} = \frac{3}{4}$
6. $\frac{10}{11}$
7. $\frac{9}{10}$
8. $\frac{4}{5}$

Teacher check work on this section.

9. $1\frac{1}{6}$
10. $\frac{7}{8}$
11. $1\frac{1}{12}$
12. $\frac{7}{8}$
13. $1\frac{4}{15}$
14. $\frac{7}{12}$
15. $\frac{7}{8}$
16. $1\frac{2}{8}$
17. $\frac{9}{12} = \frac{3}{4}$
18. $1\frac{5}{14}$
19. $1\frac{1}{10}$
20. $1\frac{1}{9}$

Learning to Subtract Fractions-p. 82

1. $\frac{4}{8} = \frac{1}{2}$
2. $\frac{4}{8} = \frac{1}{2}$
3. $\frac{7}{16}$
4. $\frac{2}{4} = \frac{1}{2}$
5. $\frac{5}{12}$
6. $\frac{6}{11}$
7. $\frac{5}{10} = \frac{1}{2}$
8. $\frac{2}{5}$

Teacher check work on this section.

9. $\frac{1}{6}$
10. $\frac{1}{8}$
11. $\frac{5}{12}$
12. $\frac{1}{8}$
13. $\frac{1}{15}$
14. $\frac{1}{12}$
15. $\frac{3}{8}$
16. $\frac{1}{9}$
17. $\frac{1}{12}$
18. $\frac{5}{14}$
19. $\frac{3}{10}$
20. $\frac{4}{9}$

**Learning to Add
Improper Fractions-
p. 83**
1. 4
2. 3
3. 3
4. $2\frac{4}{8} = 2\frac{1}{2}$
5. 4
6. $2\frac{4}{5}$
7. $2\frac{3}{4}$
8. $2\frac{2}{8} = 2\frac{1}{4}$
9. $2\frac{1}{10}$

**Reviewing Addition
and Subtraction of
Fractions-p. 83**
1. $1\frac{4}{8} = 1\frac{1}{2}$
2. $1\frac{2}{3}$
3. $3\frac{1}{3}$
4. $1\frac{2}{6} = 1\frac{1}{3}$
5. $\frac{7}{4}$
6. $\frac{10}{3}$
7. $\frac{11}{4}$
8. $\frac{41}{8}$
9. $\frac{2}{8} = \frac{1}{4}$
10. $\frac{7}{7} = 1$
11. $\frac{6}{9} = \frac{2}{3}$
12. $\frac{4}{4} = 1$
13. $2\frac{3}{5}$
14. $3\frac{2}{12} = 3\frac{1}{6}$
15. $2\frac{1}{4}$
16. $2\frac{5}{6}$

**Whole Numbers Times
Fractions-p. 84**
1. $1\frac{2}{3}$
2. $2\frac{2}{3}$
3. 6
4. 3
5. $5\frac{1}{3}$
6. 9
7. $3\frac{3}{5}$
8. $1\frac{1}{5}$
9. $2\frac{1}{4}$
10. $1\frac{1}{6}$

**Fractions Times
Whole Numbers-p. 84**
1. 9
2. 4
3. 10
4. $6\frac{2}{3}$
5. $3\frac{3}{8}$
6. 4
7. 10
8. $1\frac{4}{8} = 1\frac{1}{2}$

9. 9
10. $4\frac{2}{4} = 4\frac{1}{2}$

**Multiplying Fractions
Times Fractions-p. 85**
1. $\frac{1}{6}$
2. $\frac{3}{12} = \frac{1}{4}$
3. $\frac{6}{12} = \frac{1}{2}$
4. $\frac{1}{15}$
5. $\frac{3}{10}$
6. $\frac{8}{15}$
7. $\frac{3}{40}$
8. $\frac{12}{35}$
9. $\frac{6}{24} = \frac{1}{4}$
10. $\frac{4}{10} = \frac{2}{5}$
11. $\frac{5}{24}$
12. $\frac{14}{72} = \frac{7}{36}$

**Multiplying Mixed
Numbers-p. 85**
Teacher check work on
this section.
1. $2\frac{1}{5}$
2. $3\frac{8}{9}$
3. $4\frac{1}{3}$
4. $4\frac{4}{9}$
5. $1\frac{4}{5}$
6. $8\frac{1}{3}$
7. $2\frac{1}{10}$
8. $7\frac{1}{9}$
9. $2\frac{1}{10}$
10. $9\frac{1}{10}$

**Learning About
Dividing Fractions-
p. 86**
Teacher check work on
this section.
1. $1\frac{2}{7}$; $\frac{3}{7}$
2. $\frac{4}{5}$; $\frac{2}{5}$
3. $\frac{12}{4} = 3$; $\frac{3}{4}$
4. $\frac{2}{8} = \frac{1}{4}$; $\frac{1}{8}$
5. $\frac{6}{3} = 2$; $\frac{2}{3}$
6. $\frac{20}{8} = 2\frac{4}{8} = 2\frac{1}{2}$; $\frac{5}{8}$
7. $\frac{6}{10} = \frac{3}{5}$; $\frac{3}{10}$
8. $\frac{14}{18} = \frac{7}{9}$; $\frac{2}{3}$
9. $\frac{14}{6} = 2\frac{2}{6} = 2\frac{1}{3}$; $\frac{2}{3}$
10. $\frac{20}{9} = 2\frac{2}{9}$; $\frac{5}{9}$
11. $\frac{9}{10}$; $\frac{3}{10}$
12. $\frac{21}{24} = \frac{7}{8}$; $\frac{3}{4}$

**Learning About Deci-
mals-p. 87-88**
1. 0.6
2. 0.75
3. 0.833

4. 0.5
5. 0.25
6. 0.625
7. 1.6
8. 0.08
9. 7.1
10. 7.10
11. 107.67
12. 432.007
13. 0.056
14. 1,073.4
15. 0.003
16. 3.99
17. 0.37
18. 26.036
19. 1,803.558
20. 0.31
21. 11.4
22. 44.91
23. 2.51
24. 9.10
25. 10.35
26. 0.0225
27. 0.8694
28. 0.536
29. 1,670.1519
30. 0.4
31. 0.20
32. 4
33. 2.1